Making Sense of Lifelong Learning

Lifelong learning is a phrase often used and discussed by those working in colleges, higher education institutions, local authorities, and by the Government, yet it seems few people really agree on what it means and the scope it covers.

This comprehensive book looks into the broad issue of lifelong learning, identifying the different ways it can be interpreted and considering the reasons why lifelong learning appears to be shunned by some. The book looks at different ways in which lifelong learning can be introduced into society, recognising that it does not just have to be through formal training and courses in educational institutions for skill enhancements.

Within the wider context of theories behind lifelong learning the author pays particular attention to:

- evolving practice
- finding the missing learners
- encouraging wider participation.

Making Sense of Lifelong Learning will be a valuable resource for anyone involved in developing adult education in universities, colleges, community centres and local authorities. It should also prove useful for staff and students on postgraduate courses which focus on issues of lifelong learning.

Norman Evans is a Visiting Professor at Goldsmiths College, University of London, and a trustee of the Learning from Experience Trust.

Making Sense of Lifelong Learning

Respecting the needs of all

Norman Evans

rf RoutledgeFalmer
Taylor & Francis Group

LONDON AND NEW YORK

First published 2003
by RoutledgeFalmer
11 New Fetter Lane, London EC4P 4EE

Simultaneously published in the USA and Canada
by RoutledgeFalmer
29 West 35th Street, New York, NY 10001

RoutledgeFalmer is an imprint of the Taylor & Francis Group

© 2003 Norman Evans

Typeset in Baskerville by Wearset Ltd, Boldon, Tyne and Wear
Printed and bound in Great Britain by Biddles Ltd, Guildford and
King's Lynn

British Library Cataloguing in Publication Data
A catalogue record for this book is available from the British
Library

Library of Congress Cataloging in Publication Data
Evans, Norman, 1923–
   Making sense of lifelong learning : respecting the needs of all / Norman Evans.
      p. cm.
   Includes bibliographical references and index.
   1. Continuing education–Great Britain. 2. Adult learning–Great Britain. I. Title.

   LC5256.G7E923 2003
   374'.941–dc21

                                                              2002044730

ISBN 0–415–28043–5 (hbk)
ISBN 0–415–28044–3 (pbk)

For Rachael, Richard, Harriet, Mark.
Learners all

Contents

Acknowledgements   viii

1 Introduction   1

2 Lifelong learning: paradox, contradiction, rediscovery   5

3 Evolving practice of lifelong learning   16

4 Catching up: who are the missing learners?   53

5 Motivational mismatches for lifelong learning   69

6 Towards wider participation: encouraging it   95

7 Widening participation – doing it: government leading
   from the front   128

8 Postscript: making sense of lifelong learning   156

References   160
Index   163

Acknowledgements

Writing a book like this towards the end of a long life spent in schools, colleges and universities and, more latterly, in the Learning from Experience Trust concentrating on the border zone between formal and informal learning, inevitably means that whatever is in it stems from experiences, ideas and dreams, stimulated professionally and personally by innumerable colleagues, friends, pupils and students. During the past twenty years regular visits to the USA, and several to South Africa and New Zealand, have added to that store, especially through many in the Chicago-based Council for Adult and Experiential Learning, colleagues who teach continuing education seminars in Cambridge and the New School in New York, and who teach in the School of New Resources, College of New Rochelle and University College, University of Maryland.

However, a few are worthy of special mention. Colin Griffin of Hillcroft College and the University of Surrey has been influential not only for this book but more generally over the years through countless conversations. Malcolm Barry, Director of the College of London, London Metropolitan University, always had penetrating comments to make based on his long experience of running Professional and Community Education at Gold-smiths College. Anne Rumpus, Head of the Educational Initiative Centre in the University of Westminster, invariably had an interesting slant to offer based on her experience of staff development. There are all the people who worked in the Learning from Experience Trust and Patrick Coldstream, formerly Director of the Council for Industry and Higher Education, with whom there have been almost bimonthly evening meetings on the topic. And who could fail to be influenced in this field by Richard Hoggart?

Above all I have been privileged to work closely for twenty years with the late Sir Charles Carter, a wise, incisive Chairman at the Trust until his death in 2002, and my good friend Morris Keeton, Founding President of the Council for Adult and Experiential Learning, who set me off on the experiential learning trail in 1979. With mentors like this, who could ask for more?

Chapter 1

Introduction

When a friend heard that I was trying to write this book, he asked whether I was going to look again at *Post Education Society* which I wrote in 1984. He believed its theme might be a useful background to whatever I had to say. So I looked at it. Its subtitle was *Recognising Adults as Learners.*

'Motivation is the key to all learning', I read. This is so obvious that I wondered why I ever wrote it. But then 'If we need to know something we are likely to learn it. However if we are capable of learning, it is not only a consequence of intelligence and training but of our level of personal development.' That is not quite so obvious.

Transposed to society, the theme was that if we managed to recognise adults as learners because they needed to know something, then we needed adult institutions to serve them. And the consequence of this was that institutions of all kinds, not merely educational ones, needed to grow into adulthood in the latter part of the twentieth century leaving their nineteenth-century adolescence behind them. Here I am trying to take the argument further and in the context of lifelong learning.

In summary the argument is that lifelong learning may be seen as an elaborate game of catch-up. In so many ways where we are is not where we ought to be. Policies that are intended to enable us to get to where we ought to be do not seem to be getting us there. It is almost as if the best efforts result in our running to stay where we are. When combined, the themes of the book are attempts to suggest how the idea of catch-up from behind could become caught up somewhere near where we need lifelong learning to be.

Now into the twenty-first century, for post education society read multinational/global society, but cautiously, because the words have become an all-purpose mantra. There is nothing new about a global economy. What is new is the reach, influence and power of multinational corporations to affect governments, countries, occupations, individuals and families. Nevertheless, whatever it is called, in a sense we now have a Post Education Society in capital letters and writ large. The need for adults to learn more has intensified as lives have become increasingly complicated and hence the need for adult institutions has become more urgent. *This is one theme which runs through the book; the need for institutions which are adult and able to serve people as adults.*

That sounds like lifelong learning. But this runs right into a paradox. For all the government's urging the case for lifelong learning, it seeks to promote it through educational institutions which were invented in the nineteenth century. For the twenty-first century they seem adolescent. They reflect the industrial society which spawned them. Many still feel rather like the factories which used to surround them. But they were all of a piece with the society they were there to serve. Now we need adult institutions.

There is now a disjunction between many of those institutions and the adults they are expected to attract. If they are to serve well the adult learners of today and tomorrow they have to organise themselves so as to reflect contemporary society with its plethora of electronic communications systems; the high standard of design beamed relentlessly through television for every conceivable item in domestic, working or holiday life; the instant gratification expectations induced through supermarkets and the entire service and entertainment industries. They have to try to keep up with what is happening in people's homes throughout the land. *Hence a second theme is the mismatch between individual adult educational and learning needs and educational institutions.*

Moreover, by concentrating on economic arguments for seeking to promote lifelong learning to strengthen the economy, which is understandable enough, governments risk ignoring other aspects of life which are of paramount importance for individuals, and hence for politicians' own constituents. *This leads to the third theme; the problems caused by a too narrow interpretation of the economic purposes of lifelong learning.*

Unfortunately this means that at many levels there is an almost fatal mismatch between government intentions and the reality of day-to-day living for millions of people. By default and with the best of intentions the mismatch is emphasised.

This becomes a matter of huge significance because governments have decreasing influence over the economies of their own countries as power has shifted from government to multinationals in a global economy. Their best efforts to prescribe for people what kinds of things they need to know are bound to be deficient. In addition, global multinationals and home-grown superstores appear to treat adults as adults through offering them ever-widening ranges of choices with more and more information about the products available. In practice, most advertisements and many cut-price blandishments treat adults like children. Too often choice is not what it seems. And politicians are not much better; they too tend to treat adults as children by avoiding open public debate on some of the controversial issues which affect people's lives, and instead stick to anodyne trivia. Thus not only do we have educational institutions that are rarely organised specifically to meet the needs of adults as learners, but there is also a general set of attitudes throughout society which preaches to adults but does not take them seriously. Apparently choice is a good thing for shopping and travel, but not for learning. What is wrong with adults deciding what they want to learn and planning with tutors how to learn it? Student-generated curriculum. *Thus a further theme is that the curriculum contributes to the mismatch between learning needs and institutions. This mismatch strikes at the heart of lifelong learning.*

One consequence of all this is that while it becomes increasingly important for people to be able to organise their own lives in rapidly changing circumstances, there is an uncomfortably widespread apathetic attitude to political matters as the means whereby people can influence how they are able to live their own lives. This assumes even greater importance as the gap widens between two sections of the population: the rich and relatively well-off and the poor.

Behind all this lies the pronounced tendency for individuals to withdraw into themselves, distancing themselves from anything which looks like community or wider connections with other people. This seems true at all levels. Ask anyone in the charitable world in London about the problems of getting trustees to serve as part of a charity's governance and they will explain that the kind of people in the City who used to be dedicated volunteers to support boys' clubs or community associations now work such long hours under such high pressure to earn while the going is good that whatever their inclinations they simply do not have the time to attend meetings, let alone the mental energy to play a significant role. Think of the individual family outings to supermarkets as replacements for the hobnobbing which used to go on in local shops in the high street. Or television. Think of the number of television sets in houses with young children and adolescents, the hours spent watching often solitarily, and the fewer and fewer occasions when everyone in a family sits down together for a meal. Then ask the question: How far is all that connected with apathy not merely of political matters, elections, debates and so on, but about what is happening to the world we live in and what is happening to ourselves and our children? From this perspective, lifelong learning attached to economic issues seems a rather puny version of what it should be about.

Another theme therefore is the complex mismatch between policies which seek to promote mass provision of lifelong learning and the lives of millions of people in an increasingly individualised society. This coincides unhappily with what appears to be a steady withdrawal in increasing numbers from any form of political activity. At worst this is an aspect of social exclusion. But the gap is made more dramatic by the government's attempts to use micromanagement to oversee the implementation of its policies. *This leads to the theme: the folly of over-centralisation and attempted control by the centre.*

So, put differently, lifelong learning may be described as an elaborate game of catch-up for policies and institutions, and to refocus on individuals to try to get to where we ought to be. Putting the themes together makes the following points: the need for adults to be treated as adults; the mismatch between individuals' learning needs and educational institutions; a too narrow interpretation of the vocational strand in lifelong learning; policies for a mass provision in an individualised society; and over-bureaucratic centralisation. It amounts to an overall critique which claims that at all levels for most considerations about lifelong learning there is a glaring mismatch between the rhetoric and exhortation by government and the reality of the way people lead their lives.

Lifelong learning should take centre stage in this scene. It is good that the government seeks to place it so. It will succeed only if there are convincingly articulated answers to two questions which each and every adult is entitled to ask. Why is it important for adults to learn more? How can existing arrangements for adults to learn more themselves mature into adulthood? If these two questions could be answered, and answered publicly and broadcast widely, then what adults learn and lifelong learning would look after itself.

Chapter 2

Lifelong learning

Paradox, contradiction, rediscovery

There is something very odd about the current debate on lifelong learning. What it is, what it is for and why it is so important, receive ambivalent answers. Looking at some of the paradoxes and contradictions may help to clarify it through rediscovery of some of the essentials. Rediscovery means examining the effect on lifelong learning of government's creeping central-isation, its heavy concentration of the vocational as an economic booster, the obstacles of participation and thinking again about the role of lifelong learning in a democracy troubled by low and declining participation.

The oddity is that it is almost as if the politicians and the advisers close to them speak and write as though they have discovered something brand new. So when lifelong learning gets trotted out at the flick of a switch it is almost as if it is proclaiming that something new is happening. At one level this is not so; it is as old as the hills. It is called informal learning. There seems a reluctance to recognise the significance of anything which is not done through formal learning. At another level whatever the reasons for hoisting lifelong learning as an educational banner, there is little sign that its implications have been thought through. There is no clear concept of lifelong learning in policy documents. Yet at another level still the very fact that there is so much attention being paid to lifelong learning means that something different is happening. No one is quite clear what.

In his 1996 lecture entitled 'Recognising the value of informal learn-ing' given at Goldsmiths College to mark The European Year of Lifelong Learning (Carter 1996), the late Sir Charles Carter warned:

> But beware of sloppy thinking. Lifelong learning ought to have no significance as an object of policy for it is like lifelong breathing – something which we cannot avoid while remaining conscious. . . . what is the proper object of 'improving the quality of lifelong learning experience?'

He went on to comment on the difficulty of thinking about lifelong learn-ing other than in formal and institutional terms. He was pointing the way to the need for rediscovery.

According to the *OED*, discover means 'to find out, or detect or light upon or suddenly realise as result of search or inquiry or accident'. Rediscover, then, means going back to have another look, thinking again. And for lifelong learning there needs to be rethinking by government about its devotion to centralisation, its concentration on the vocational interpretation of lifelong learning and the impact of its activities on democracy itself, seen against the present paradoxes and contradictions.

Much of this comes later, but for a start rediscovery means peering into three areas in particular: informal learning; schools as launching pads for lifelong learning, and the changing context of work. Together these illustrate the contradictions between attempts to promote lifelong learning and real people's lives and their consequences for motivation to learn.

Informal learning

First, informal learning. To begin at the beginning: the fact is that continual learning is a condition of human survival to differing degrees, at different levels in different parts of the world. Darwin will not be denied. No parent teaches a small baby how to crawl. Whether the child crawls in a crab-like style or on hands and knees is simply because that child has hit on the best means of propulsion. And when the child is about to collide with a chair leg, a toy-box or even the cat, and the parent shouts 'Mind out. Not that way. Be careful', even though the child does not know what the words mean, a bump on the head is useful learning. Bump, tears, cuddle, smile and off we go again. But something has been learned and there was no script for it. Noise and tone, like that loud voice, signals trouble ahead. At the other end of life elderly people manage to cope with their frailties by living within the constraints which age has imposed on them. But in common parlance neither what the small child nor what the elderly person does counts as learning. Parents learn fast too, never mind books on child-rearing. This can be extended into all the learning that goes on in families, and with friends and neighbours. What is the best top dressing to get the best broad beans? How to deal with the self-assessment forms for income tax? Choosing between different curtain fabrics by weighing up their respective weights, cleaning and washing instructions, and how quickly they would fade. All this is learning, and it is transferred effortlessly from one context to another. It is learning but not recognised as such, because it does not fit the way formal education provision is organised. It is informal learning. It is invisible. Its results may be highly visible.

Informal learning falls into two obvious broad categories. There is informal learning which comes from things which cannot be avoided, such as being alive, or suffering from a disease, or recovering from some disaster, or following the routine of the workaday world, things over which we have little or no control. That is one category. Then there is informal learning which we choose to undertake, such as following an OU course without registering for it, or reading up on DIY, or using a reference book to classify butterflies or joining a health club. That is the other category of informal learning. The first is done to us. The second is something we choose to do for ourselves.

There is informal learning which comes incidentally, unexpectedly and more often than not unrecognised from the various activities which are planned. Holiday plans, fishing competitions, new ways of cooking, all can be planned meticulously but without any deliberate intention of learning anything over and above the immediate requirements for getting the job done, whatever it is. Then there are all the voluntary and community activities. The secretary of the village hall committee may become very knowledgeable about planning and building regulations. Treasurers may learn a lot from their auditors. Governors of schools have to learn a lot about their legal obligations. None of them set out to learn from what they volunteer to do. But in many cases, learn they do. And when they do it is because of what they have chosen to do.

But neither category of informal learning rates as learning as seen by government or formal education, simply because it is all taken for granted. It is certainly taken for granted by the child, the elderly person and onlookers, and in reality both child and ageing grandparent act the way they do because they want to. Of course they did not sit there and debate internally 'Now I may be going to crawl', or 'I shall not attempt to walk too fast for that bus'. They just do it. But each has a motive for what they do. So with all informal learning, whatever its source; it is either imposed or undertaken for particular reasons. Motivation is the key to learning, whether formal or informal. Common sense says so. But so does any theory of learning.

Motivation

Down the ages, people have always had motivation to learn. The essential difference is between the ways people learned what they needed to learn at different periods. When priests and lawyers needed documents, whether religious or secular, scribes mastered the skills to do the necessary copying and record-keeping. Apart from the courts, monasteries and later grammar schools and Inns of Court for the few, up until the Industrial Revolution, most learning was in the oral tradition of one generation handing its knowledge and skill down to a succeeding generation through apprenticeships, or by watching, listening and doing on a trial-and-error pattern, often with a cuff over the ears. Informal learning, no less. When the Industrial Revolution created mass populations in towns and cities, learning moved into a formal mass institutional stage to man the factories and all the clerical work in offices that went with them. Schools resembling factories came on the scene and were organised like them to provide the growing number of clerks equipped with the levels of literacy and numeracy required to keep the industrial wheels turning and the chimneys smoking. But this was not available to everyone and it changed only slowly. In 1891 10-year-olds were still sent down the mines. Later, technicians and mechanics were needed for the same reason and so institutions were created to supply them. International trade increased that need. Formal learning boomed. So it goes on; and as it has gone on, the tendency to assume that education is the same as learning has become entrenched.

For the past 150 years or so there have been continual complaints that the country was lagging behind others because of poor scientific and technological provision for learning. There always followed erratic efforts to boost economic performance through providing more technical education, more formal learning. Then there was no doubt about the motivation of the learners. At the most basic level they learned so as to survive, and above that it was to sustain incomes and a good standard of living. Of course, at every stage of introducing increasingly formal arrangements for that learning which involved expenditure by the state, there was wide political controversy about the dangers of educating too many people. But with the need compelling, in time, it was met steadily but surely. There was no difficulty in making sense of that sort of learning.

During the past fifty years it is as if that motivation can no longer be counted on. The work ethic has relaxed its grip. A consumer grip has replaced it. Former rules do not apply. So the common sense of learning has become fractured and more difficult to recognise even as it has become more necessary. There has been a gamut of innovations to increase the level of knowledge and skill in larger numbers of people, but there has always been a heavy emphasis on what has come to be called the vocational. And that misuse of the word indicates neatly the paradox which lifelong learning has created for itself. Vocation used to mean some personal dedication in attitude to whatever occupation it was, whether the church, teaching, medicine, the law and so on. And there were craftsmen. Highly skilled carpenters were proud of their calling to be craftsmen and of the public recognition that went with it. Now in lifelong learning 'vocational' refers primarily to any activity that contributes directly to the economy. Given the story of the past it is not surprising that government interprets it thus.

Government initiatives

Relatively recently emphasis on that version of the vocational has produced a succession of initiatives, assuming that the older versions of motivation were still there. There was the Open Tech, the Open College, the National Council for Vocational Qualifications, the Training and Enterprise Councils (TECs). Further Education Colleges were expanded for the same reason. Generally however, these successive innovative attempts have failed to do what they were created to do; namely to increase significantly through formal learning the number of men and women who were more knowledgeable than their predecessors. This despite the contribution made by employers to these various efforts, especially through the TECs. Now in 2002, almost simultaneously there is the replacement of the TECs by the Learning and Skills Council with its Regional Skills Councils: there is the beefing up of national training organisations; there is the rather oddly named University for Industry; there is the idea of a two-year Foundation degree, all accompanied by the rhetoric of lifelong learning. These are the latest shots in the locker. The omens are that they will struggle to be any more successful in hitting the target than their forerunners. The reason for this is that the vocational is only half the story. Adults are more than wage earners. There has to be something else to motivate them.

Inside this half story there are the attempts to devise ways of measuring the benefits of public spending in outcome terms of vocational qualifications awarded or course completion rates. Again it is entirely understandable that the government feels safer when there appears to be hard evidence of results based on publicly verifiable figures. But when that approach is adopted for assessing the quantity and quality of lifelong learning, it becomes largely a self-defeating attempt to measure the unmeasurable. These requirements of formal institutions which try to make a contribution to lifelong learning tend to inhibit their efforts, standing in the way of their serving the very people who lifelong learning ought to be helping. Like children, institutions are told what to do by their overbearing parents in Whitehall.

Not least, this approach risks offending against everything known about how people learn best. Teaching and lecturing become instruction, accompanied by sets of externally imposed instruments – tests, examinations – all expressed in terms of targets which are then consigned to performance tables. No longer can this approach be called educational; nor can it meet contemporary needs. Where earlier instruction in skills – reading, writing, calculating, technical crafts, engineering skills and now IT – would suffice, it does not do so now because behind all the rhetoric of lifelong learning in vocational terms lies the pre-eminent need to have more people who think about what they are doing and how to improve it. Encouraging people to think and go on thinking is an educational enterprise and not a matter of instruction.

Why participate?

So the basic questions posed by all the contemporary rhetoric about life-long learning are: What is the missing motive, and what could supply the motivation for individuals? That is the basic issue for public policy. Rhetoric and exhortation will not do. If people are not doing something which, for whatever reason, government wants them to do, two deductions follow: (1) they are not motivated to follow the government line; and (2) they are not motivated because they have not been convinced of the reasons offered as to why they should follow the government line. There is a contradiction somewhere. So far this represents the failure of lifelong learning.

It is very odd indeed. What is the difficulty about that half of the story? All around lies evidence of the need to know more. Global warming with all the dramatic climatic variations that are alleged to stem from it is affecting increasingly the everyday lives of people: floods, storms, seasonal upsets, transport congestion and rail safety, food science and the food chain, and BSE, GM food and crops. All call for more knowledge on the part of the general public, and increasingly awkward questions are being asked. And these questions are one route, perhaps the best route to learn-ing. But this does not get translated into versions of lifelong learning which have a vocational slant. It brings the economic model of lifelong learning into question. That disconnection has a great deal to do with the failure to touch the potential learners in the other half story. Motivation is just not there. Motivation is there when some form of informal learning is undertaken deliberately or when formal learning is undertaken by choice. This simple truth needs to be rediscovered.

Schools: preparation for lifelong learning

Then there are schools and the difficulties faced in trying to make school experience a preparation for lifelong learning. Within that half story lie some of the disquieting factors about compulsory schooling and its con-nection with lifelong learning. Despite all the efforts to enhance the levels of learning achievements for everyone in any age cohort, significant numbers of young men and women leave school thoroughly disaffected with learning as a whole, with many of them convinced that they are fail-ures as learners. Ofsted has made some contribution to overall standards, but these efforts are hampered by some elements in the centralised National Curriculum and under its first Chief Inspector, by its unfortunate denigration of teachers. Government is now taking this very seriously and pouring millions into secondary schools, ring-fenced as Excellence in Cities, Beacon Schools, technology status and increased devolution of funding and expenditure.

Nevertheless, 30,000 young people left school in July 2002 without any qualification at all. In a report published by the Prince's Trust, Tom Shebbeare, its Chief Executive, says:

> Exam result season is meant to be a joyous time, but for young people leaving school without qualifications it may be the beginning of a life time struggle to find work.

Not that qualifications are the be all and end all, but they are an indication of achievement and point to the catch-up problem.

In an odd and uncomfortable way this repeats the problem of catching up with skill deficiencies. The Newsom Report of 1963, *Half our Future*, galvanised many a local education authority and countless schools into developing schemes designed to engage those young men and women who were unlikely to feature in examination stakes. With the school-leaving age due to go up to 16 from 15, more buildings were planned, and curricula took on some truly innovative developments designed deliberately to engage young people. The Humanities Project led by Lawrence Stenhouse with his brilliant team including Barry Macdonald, Jean Ruddock and John Elliott demonstrated conclusively that not only could those young people in what were then predominantly secondary modern schools learn effectively and at good levels through discussion of topics which concerned them as members of society, but that it was far more effective than the traditional didactic methods. What was then called the Extended Day was developed widely as well. This amounted to a properly staffed range of extra-curricula activities. *Half our Future* created a climate in which the curricula of schools and their after-school offerings could be tuned to the needs of that half of the school population which *Half our Future* had described. Many a school became a place of enthusiasm for learning. Many staff had a sense of being part of exciting developments. Many pupils found that learning was not bad after all. In many cases the division between formal and informal learning was blurred.

However, this was all stopped in its tracks. The financial problems of the Labour government from 1964 to 1968 caused public funds for school buildings to be slashed and the raising of the school-leaving age was postponed. In fact it waited for twenty years. As a result, generations of young people went through schools which were unable to realise the beneficial school experience which the Newsom Report had recommended. Instead, hundreds of thousands of schoolchildren became bored, disillusioned and could not wait to walk out through the school gates for the last time. Worse still, outside the school during those twenty years those selfsame young people were affected by the rapid changes in social and economic life. Progressively youth unemployment gained a grip on increasing numbers, devastatingly so in some parts of the country. For them, school seemed a pretty pointless business, as did the various youth training schemes. What was the point of training for jobs which were not there? There were not enough jobs to go around. Where employment had served as a rite of passage to adulthood, for many there was just emptiness, even hopelessness. These are the generations who are now being urged to become enthusiastic about lifelong learning. The tragedy is that thirty or so years ago, there were signs that secondary schools were developing curricula approaches which might have helped to minimise the impact of those national factors on their young adult students.

All this has backed up into the schools themselves. In many staff rooms morale sank alongside that of their pupils. Teacher-bashing became something of a political sport as they got blamed for serving pupils poorly in circumstances which were not of their making. Unemployment was not the fault of teachers. Resources were so inadequate that school buildings and premises were neglected disgracefully. Pay was poor. For something like 50 per cent of the secondary school population learning and education became a depressed area.

Now enthusiasm for lifelong learning is not something which can be turned on at will. There has to be something in a person's perception of the world and his or her place in it which makes further learning either necessary or enjoyable, or in some way desirable. Patently the school experience of hundreds of thousands and their early experience of the adult world has been no seed-bed for growing enthusiasms for further learning in any formal setting.

Fast-forward thirty-five years or more from Newsom, and men and women now aged 20 to 50 without many qualifications are represented heavily among those who are supposed to be filling up the vocational courses offered beneath a lifelong learning banner. It is little surprise to find that they do not flock to enrolment evenings, particularly in a period of dramatically rising standards of living, with holidays abroad being the norm for huge sections of the population.

So just as previous efforts to jack up levels of technical competence tended to be too late in the day to be effective as and when required to keep the economy healthy, namely attempted catch-ups, so the current efforts to raise the level of learning achievements in secondary schools and provide a better, richer preparation for the world of work are but late attempts to catch up with where schools and their pupils ought to be in the world where they live.

For both the adult world and secondary education, these efforts may be seen as catch-up exercises in their different ways. A large part of the trouble is that a great deal of secondary education as construed at present is not an effective launching pad for after-school engagement with lifelong learning. This is what some of the debate about lifelong learning amounts to. Thus the question is: If it is so important, what is it that can make a difference? And that begins to touch on the other half of the story. It focuses attention on the possible connections between informal learning and what schools are allowed to do.

A different world

Then there is the changing world in which the potential learners for lifelong learning actually live. The context for thinking about any form of post-school earning has changed so dramatically over the past twenty-five years that whatever it is that can make a difference has changed too; and necessarily so. Every conceivable aspect of society is different from what it was a relatively short time ago. Work, home, family, leisure, and all the adult roles within them, are as different as chalk from cheese. It all tells the same tale. More and more people are taking more responsibility for what happens in their own lives as they live them, taking a greater interest in matters which can affect them, from food, how to grow it, shop for it, cook it, eat it to global warming, from obesity to artificial insemination. What is more, the opportunities for people to learn have expanded exponentially. Television, radio, Web access is now available to knowledge and information for huge numbers of people who want it. And the shelves of self-help books in bookshops, hot lines for a range of people who are in distress for one reason or another, all point in the same direction. Learning has become a personal activity for individuals as never before. What is more, the sheer range of topics on any list of what people are learning these days would have seemed inconceivable to former generations. But perhaps the most important aspect of all this is that most people would not describe what they are doing as learning as they seek to master whatever topic they engage with. But learning is precisely what they are doing. It writes the other half of the story. It goes back to informal learning.

To some extent these developments are a mirror image of what has happened to employment. Jobs for life have all but gone entirely. Moving through a number of different jobs or even different areas of employment during a working lifetime is what more and more men and women find themselves doing at all levels of employment, including the professions. A portfolio of jobs is the trendy way of putting it. This argues for a huge increase in the personal responsibility exercised by people going through that experience of employment. Inevitably that experience of taking personal responsibility will be applied to other aspects of life.

One result of these developments and shifts in society, especially the changing pattern of employment, is that attempts to think of lifelong learning on a bulk provision basis collide with the way more and more people are actually living out their lives. For many, portfolios of employment fit better alongside a personal pick-and-mix approach to any further learning which may be undertaken rather than formal courses listed in a college prospectus. The woman who pores over the *BBC Good Food Magazine* in wrapt attention as she works through a likely looking set of ingredients and what to do with them is unlikely to attend formal classes designed to make her a more productive employee unless she had thought of it for herself in the first place. Nor is the man who spends all his non-working hours as a volunteer engineer, rebuilding steam locomotives to put them in working order for, say, the Festiniog Railway, going to take kindly to being told that in order to improve his performance at ASDA, he needs to attend a course on computerising inventories when that is what he has to do in his volunteering time to find spare parts.

It is this tension between plans for boosting lifelong learning through formal institutions and the way people are now leading their lives which so far does not seem to have been taken into consideration when White Papers appear for discussion as forerunners to Acts of Parliament. Indeed, it is almost ironic how lifelong learning is used in the rhetoric as something which can help sustain a coherent society when much of that society is moving in the opposite direction. It is as if the increasing individualisation of society is happening somewhere else. But it is not. It is here with us now. It is another contradiction. And it is hard to see why this tendency will not grow stronger, leading to changes in society which can only be guessed at. There could be a premium on connections between flourishing lifelong learning and a healthy democracy.

This is perhaps why public rhetoric does not get transposed in public action which is tuned to present circumstances. Perhaps tackling that tension is too hot an issue for politicians to grapple with. Cynics might say that just as schooling can be interpreted over the years as a means of exerting a form of social control, so talking about lifelong learning in terms of formal provision which is under tight control by government may also be a covert and perhaps nervous way of trying to do the same things with adults. If so, then lifelong learning could turn out to contain some rather inconvenient social time bombs. Subsequently there could be a great deal of rediscovery.

Perhaps, too, there is a simpler explanation: that for all its good intentions the government has no clear idea of what it believes lifelong learning to mean. So many phrases get bandied around. Sometimes there is the 'true purpose of learning', the 'attitude to learning'. It would be an interesting exercise to set a test for the civil servants responsible for the use of these phrases, requiring them to articulate clearly the meaning of each one of them and to describe the differences which those meanings are intended to convey.

This muddled thinking could rest on what Sally Tomlinson claims about education change in general:

There is also confusion about political focus and ideological purpose behind educational change. This is partly due to a rhetoric that the state has given more freedom to individuals while in reality central control has tightened.

(Tomlinson 2001)

Rediscovery

But behind any such confusion lies the basic issue of motivation. It has to be rediscovered. It may be true that everyone has a teacher lurking somewhere within them. It is certainly not true that everyone has an internal switch labelled 'get learning' somewhere waiting to be thrown. Lifelong learning cannot be turned on at will. Enthusiasm for learning comes when there is some reason to learn, whether it is necessary for employability or fear of unemployment, a way of getting additional enjoyment, escaping into another world or just thoroughly desirable. Informal learning which is a chosen pursuit generates enthusiasm because people have chosen to pursue it. Motivation is integral to the undertaking. If young students could leave school with some sense of the importance, the significance of their own informal learning, then some might generate some motivation for wanting more of it. But any questioning about motivation has to be conducted against the background of a complex world in which governments are just as likely to find confusion as individuals.

All these factors, namely informal learning, vocational training, the problems of schools, the changing context for work and life – illustrate the contradictions which lie between so-called policies for lifelong learning and the real lives of people and their consequences for motivation. But so long as prime emphasis is on the economic rationale for lifelong learning, whatever the needs for training and retraining, motivation is bound to be patchy. As long as informal learning is seen as a poor relation to formal learning and schools remain in their relatively antediluvian posture, motivation is unlikely to be tapped.

Sir Charles Carter again:

> Bringing up a family induces far more learning than attending an evening class; where are our programmes for improving the quality of that learning and for enabling parents to learn from their mistakes?
>
> (Carter 1996)

The rediscovery of lifelong learning means mounting a search as wide as the people themselves and their society for what they want to learn, where and how.

Chapter 3

Evolving practice of lifelong learning

This could be a very long story from the beginnings of mankind, but as part of the rediscovery of some of the essentials about lifelong learning it is a second half of the twentieth-century story.

Long before governments took an interventionist interest in lifelong learning, voluntary organisations were offering all manner of opportunities for adults to learn. In some ways their success makes them exemplars of how to develop lifelong learning successfully, but with one essential difference. Until comparatively recently, qualifications and credentials were of scant interest to them. The people who came to them wanted to learn and they lived in a world where formal education qualifications for adults concerned only a minority. However, as the decades passed and the immediate post-Second World War period was left behind, economic problems crept up with increasing speed so that governments felt impelled to take positive steps to improve levels of skill and knowledge in the workforce as they worried about the overall health of the economy. Employers needed as highly skilled employees as they could find to sustain their productivity. Individuals needed to try to keep themselves employable. Lifelong learning acquired a heavy vocational emphasis.

It therefore moved from R.H. Tawney's vision of taking university-level learning to ordinary people without a thought of examinations to the government's newest initiative to promote lifelong learning, namely the Learning and Skills Council with the full panoply of regulatory funding and monitoring equipment, to underpin the drive for accredited courses so as to provide the country with the employees needed to enable employers to succeed in the global economy. As its name implies, and its mission states, contributing to the enhancement of the economy is its top priority.

The assessment of prior experiential learning

During the past twenty-five years there has been another development which has sharpened the focus on informal learning: a growing interest in the assessment of prior experiential learning. This is now fast becoming something of an international phenomenon. But in this country few influences can have had the same impact on the thinking about and the possibilities offered in lifelong learning as the way in which the assessment of prior and experiential learning (APEL) has established itself as a reputable activity within post-secondary education in further education, colleges and universities. In post-secondary education it was an important way of indicating that adults could be treated as adults. It underlined the significance of the informal. Beginning in 1980 the practice of APEL has spread steadily.

The first to take it up were the polytechnics and colleges of higher education under active encouragement from the Council for National Academic Awards. Further education became involved as adult educators saw its potential for developing access courses, often in collaboration with the nearest polytechnic. As the government sought to persuade universities to put greater emphasis on the potential employability of their students, a whole range of projects were funded by the Department of Employment under the heading of Work-based Learning, which derives from the assessment of experiential learning. In addition, since work-based learning projects necessarily had to be developed in collaboration with employers, APEL began to seep into the consciousness of some in the world of work. APEL prompted additional ways of thinking about learning and how adults learn, and so this became integral to lifelong learning.

This is not to claim that APEL can be seen to be active in institutions and work places up and down the country, but it has spread modestly. And where it has spread, it has done so because of what it is. APEL is based on the assertion that many people acquire significant learning through their work whatever it may be, their leisure, hobbies and travel, whether it is gardening, DIY, fishing, or what is loosely called sightseeing, television and radio programmes, and private reading, as well as formal courses which are not part of qualification programmes. Informal learning from work, community, family life, independent learning, museums, fun and games, whether as intentional learning by personal choice and/or accidental through some other activity, all of it has the potential for generating identifiable learning. It also asserts that when some of that learning is identified, articulated and organised into clear statements of claims for knowledge and skill, it can be recognised, assessed and accredited for those who want it, provided it meets the regulations of the formal course in question. This is because it frequently proves to be worthy of formal recognition in relation to a course which an individual may wish to follow.

The universities are a telling example of the spread. When the Learning from Experience Trust published *Mapping APEL: Accreditation of Prior Experiential Learning in English Higher Education* in March 2000 (LET 2000) it found that out of the 133 institutions contacted, 107 universities and colleges (80 per cent) responded to the first survey and of those some fifty-two had public institutional or departmental policies applying to APEL. Forty of those 107 then answered a detailed questionnaire about the various ways in which institutions set about dealing with APEL, and further detailed case studies rounded off the Report. Those responses the universities gave and the trouble they went to provide full replies to two sets of questions means nothing less than that APEL is a serious business in the university sector as a whole.

But APEL is not just about accreditation and assessment. APEL turns out to be a powerful education tool in its own right. The very fact of having to reflect on experience in attempting to articulate what had been learned from it means that people learn a great deal not only about themselves but they discover what was significant about the experiences they are investigating. They learn from the past. But they are also learning in the present through the activity of the reflection they undertake. Because they had taken all that for granted without knowing its significance, they may be surprised to find what they have accomplished as learners already without even realising it. For some, this can be a transforming experience, and for many again that experience of increased self-knowledge can be sufficient. They have no need of assessment for accreditation. They can rest quietly with satisfaction at what they now know themselves to be: more self-confident, with a sense of possibilities formerly not thought of but now engendered. Technically egos have been strengthened. It is a form of personal development which is central to a long-standing tradition running through adult education and extends into the full meaning of lifelong learning.

Thus, seen against demography and the changing composition of society with its widening range of perspectives, APEL offers an additional dimension to thinking about and practising lifelong learning. It challenges conventional understandings of curricula. It is just waiting there to be exploited. It is a vital factor in its evolution. Quite apart from anything else, APEL draws attention to the unsatisfactory relationship between informal learning and formal learning. Unsatisfactory, because all too often those providing formal learning in formal education institutions tend to ignore the significance of informal learning, treating it as of no account. In some ways this is understandable, though in this day and age that does not make it any the more forgivable.

This attitude is a hangover from the heavy institutionalisation of learning over the last century and a half. The nineteenth century saw a steady systematisation of the rag-bag of schools, universities, academies, colleges and institutes which had gone their idiosyncratic ways that were acceptable in the pre-industrial age, but were inadequate as engines to propel industrialisation. As requirements from the world of work fed back into the schools as curriculum prescriptions, and as reforms tidied up the way universities were run, and school systems were established and built to operate rather like factories, formal education became the accepted norm for learning. It was all that was required. And in due course this led to the assumption that formal education institutions had a monopoly of knowledge and skill and therefore of learning. This formalisation occurred elsewhere. It was part of a society which saw entry to the civil service based on publicly provided examinations replace the mysterious routes opened through private patronage. Lifelong learning as it is now officially promoted is merely the latest twist to the story of adult education and learning.

Liberal adult education

The year 2002 was not like the nineteenth century or, for that matter, the first eighty years of the twentieth century. When Winston Churchill rejected Florence Horsburgh's wish to reduce spending on adult education in 1951 he was not implying that he understood fully the connection between informal and formal learning in the way it is seen now, and his view of the relative significance of science and technology may seem antediluvian. But his magisterial statement does imply an understanding of the overall purposes of lifelong learning which is worth heeding now.

> There is perhaps no branch of our vast education system which should more attract within its particular sphere the aid and encouragement of the State than adult education. How many must there be in Britain, after the disturbance of two destructive wars, who thirst in later life to learn about the humanities, the history of their country, the philosophies of the human race and the arts and letters which sustain and are borne forward by the ever-conquering English language.
>
> This ranks in my opinion far above science and technical instruction which are well sustained and not without their reward in our present system. The mental and moral outlook of free men studying the past with free minds in order to discern the future, demands the highest measures which our hard-pressed finances can sustain. I have no doubt myself that a man or woman earnestly seeking in grown-up life to be guided to wide and suggestive knowledge in its largest and most uplifting sphere will make the best of all pupils in this age of clutter and buzz, of gape and gloat. The appetite of adults to be shown the foundations and processes of thought will never be denied by a British administration cherishing the continuity of our island life.
>
> (Hoggart 1995: 50–1)

This from a self-taught man who knew full well the value of informal learning. Whether he had heard of the Workers Education Association or the University Extension Movement matters not. The high-flown language and the exalted rationale speak to the need for healthy societies to foster learning in all possible ways. As such it did not, until very recently, fit easily alongside much of the contemporary discussion about lifelong learning, but it is not a bad yardstick to measure what we are up to fifty years later.

Straddling that choice piece of Churchilliana before and after the Second World War was the Workers Educational Association (WEA) and the University Extension Movement. Founded by Alfred Mansbridge in 1903, the WEA began as a carefully considered means of relating University Extension lectures more closely to the needs and interests of working men and women. By 1910 there were seventy branches of the WEA. Today there are about a thousand. Each branch was and is a self-governing body with voluntary officers, and it was and is the branch which decided what topics it wished to offer for study. Tutorial classes were its essential mode of study. At the beginning they were for a three-year stint studying one topic at one meeting each week. This changed over the years but the levels and standards of study remained constant. R.H. Tawney took one of the first two tutorial classes. He once reflected: 'the friendly smiting of weavers, potters, miners and engineers have taught me much about the problems of political and economic science which cannot easily be learned from books.' Both Mansbridge and Tawney worked on the assumption that many ordinary working-class people, who had left school at age 14 if not earlier (mainly men as it turned out), were perfectly capable of grappling with academic study at university level. That inspiration lasted long up and down the country. University extramural or extension departments and WEA regions were staffed by academics who believed in that assumption. This form of adult education was spurred on by the experience of the Army Bureau of Current Affairs towards the end of the war and it developed swiftly from 1946 onward.

Moreover, because of the very nature of their work with people who turned to learning voluntarily, these academics were highly skilled teachers. Whether it was history, local, social or global, geography, literature, archaeology or music they had to be good. The men and women in the classes were hungry for knowledge and understanding but if a tutor could not hold a class they simply went away. (There is a lesson here for contemporary academics in mainstream university provision.) There may have been and often was an economic social and political flavour to what some tutors understood themselves to be doing with the students but it was all at a macro level of changing social and economic systems. Understanding better the world they lived in, domestically, nationally and internationally, was what many of these volunteer learners were seeking. What is more it was a way of gaining a better understanding about their place in that world and what they could try to do to change it if they so wished. In the immediate postwar years there was a sense of possibilities even during the ration book regime and up until the early 1960s. Skills and retraining were light years away from their immediate concerns. Towering figures included Raymond Williams who both taught and edited the journal *Highway* before becoming a don at Jesus College, Cambridge; John Hampden Jackson at the Cambridge Extra-mural Board was a passionate teacher of international affairs; Frank Jacques, Secretary to the Eastern Region of the WEA, promoted classes throughout his region; Richard Hoggart's first appointment was as an assistant tutor in the Extramural Department of University College, Hull. These were among the exemplars of doing what Churchill was talking about. They knew what liberal education was, and they prosecuted it.

They knew how to prosecute it as well. The guiding pedagogical principle for tutors in WEA classes or university extension classes was as Tawney so eloquently expressed: the recognition that in any class at any place and at any time there were always likely to be class members who knew more about some aspect of the subject being studied than the tutor. Thus discussion was an essential learning tool, not idle reminiscences, but focused exchanges to explore, elucidate, and illuminate whatever the topic was, using the full resources of whoever was in the room. As a pedagogical method it was related closely to APEL.

Then there were the Cambridgeshire Village Colleges. They came on the scene during the late 1920s and 1930s. The Chief Education Officer Henry Morris had a vision of a single unit serving as a school for secondary-aged pupils during the day, and an adult education centre in the evenings. They were to be attractive buildings in their own right, adding to the facilities in a unique way which the inhabitants became extremely proud of. Henry Morris' Village Colleges were community schools designed architecturally to enable that vision to become a reality. Walter Gropius was the architect for the first College. Their influence was widespread, as one local education authority showed what could be done when it put its mind to it. The Village Colleges plotted an important step in the evolution of lifelong learning in the second half of the twentieth century.

Local education authorities had a duty to provide education services which they met in a variety of ways. For some, adult education ran through leisure services. Some had adult education officers charged with the task of developing that service. Most made extensive use of their further education colleges as vehicles both for specialised and general education. Then there was no differentiation in the arrangements for funding both vocational courses and everything else that might be lumped together as general interest which later adopted the derogatory label of 'flower arranging'.

Thus by the end of the 1930s and at the onset of war there was a wide variety of provision for what is now labelled 'lifelong learning'.

The Second World War saw a huge expansion of what in retrospect was a comprehensive programme of lifelong learning. The Army's Bureau of Current Affairs provided compulsory adult education so that serving soldiers could begin to come to terms with the civilian world they were returning to. For many, this whetted the appetite for more of the same. University extramural departments, the WEA and local education authorities expanded quickly the overall provision of adult education.

Education Permanente

Twenty years later Unesco was urging the concept of Education Permanente. In December 1965 a memorandum was adopted by the International Committee for the Advancement of Adult Education which recommended:

> Unesco should endorse the principles of lifelong education ... which may be defined briefly as the animating principle of the whole process of education, regarded as continuing throughout an individual's life from his earliest childhood to the end of his days, and therefore called for integrated organisation. The necessary integration should be achieved both vertically, throughout the duration of life, and horizontally to cover the various aspects of the life of individuals and societies.

Like a modified version of the influence spread through secondary schools by the publication of the Newsom Report, *Half our Future* in 1963, this report encouraged adult educators to run conferences to try to promote the idea: lifelong learning by another name. One such was held in 1967 at Rewley House, the headquarters of the Delegacy for Extramural Studies in the University of Oxford. Frank Jessup, Secretary to Delegates, wrote the Introduction to *Lifelong Learning: A symposium on Continuing Education* which he also edited. He said, 'it is easy to assent to this principle as an abstract proposition. It is more difficult to foresee what would be the consequences of putting it into practice' (Jessup 1969). He might just as well have been commenting on Churchill's earlier ringing declaration of faith as well as speculating about current uncertainties regarding lifelong learning.

The net was cast wide to try and assess what those consequences might be. A number of distinguished people offered their versions. Sir George Pickering, Regius Professor of Medicine, talked about 'Education for tomorrow: a biologist's view'. Jessup himself offered the Idea of lifelong learning. W.R. Elliott, Senior Chief Inspector of the Department of Education and Science, dealt with schools, colleges and universities. Cy Houle from Chicago talked of 'continuing professional education', as did

D. Lofts, Director of the Local Government Training Board. Industrial education was presented by D.W. Hutchings, Fellow in Science Education, the Education Department in Oxford University, and E.C. Goldring, Deputy Director of the Glacier Institute of Management. John Scupham, formerly Controller of Education Broadcasting at the BBC, offered a paper on 'The media of mass communication'. 'Libraries and museums' were covered by Jean M. Cook, Director of the Oxford City and County Museum, and D.E. Gerard, City Librarian, Nottingham. E.F. Bellchambers, Principal of Kingsway College, and Canon L.G. Appleton, Diocesan Director of Education, Canterbury, covered 'The voluntary associations', and The responsibilities of public authorities, was addressed by C.J. Chenevix-Trench, County Education Officer, Warwickshire. John Vaizey, Professor of Economics at Brunel University, dealt with social and economic policy, and A. Miller, former Chief Inspector for Kent and then consultant to UNESCO, summed up with 'First things first':

> It was the generosity of the W.K. Kellogg Foundation which enabled that galaxy of people to try to make sense of all those topics over a five day period. Their range is instructive. So is the range of institutions to which that list of people were affiliated. Both are a reminder of how far notions of lifelong learning have narrowed since the end of the 1950s and the 1960s.

At the time little attention was being paid to the explicit versions of lifelong learning as vocational education and training, and none at all to the formal recognition that some of the learning acquired merited academic recognition. There was no need. Adult education was a good thing; there was just not enough of it.

The Russell Report and the Advisory Committee on Adult and Continuing Education

When the Russell Report (DES 1973) was submitted in 1973, Margaret Thatcher was Secretary of State for Education and Science. A crucially important document, it explored some of the issues raised by the liberal/vocational divide in lifelong learning. It argued the case for the establishment of a Developmental Council for Adult Continuing Education. Thatcher shelved it.

When Shirley Williams became Secretary of State in the 1974 Labour government, she had behind her the frustrating experience, when she was Minister for Higher Education in a previous government, of issuing the famous thirteen points to be addressed by universities; they were ignored. The universities have paid the price for the blindness of this folly ever since. As Secretary of State Williams went straight for the target of getting something done and drew on the Russell Report. She supported adult education by establishing the Advisory Council for Adult and Continuing Education (ACACE) with Richard Hoggart as its Chairman. In 1977 this was going with the flow. Hoggart had returned from UNESCO where he had been Assistant Director-General from 1969 to 1976 to be Warden of Goldsmiths College in the University of London. In the ten years since Education Permanente was first given an airing by Unesco, increasing attention had been given to adult and continuing education; thus the two-part brief for ACACE almost wrote itself. First, it was to advise on ways of promoting co-operation between all the various bodies active in adult education, to review practice 'with a view to the most effective deployment of available resources'. But second, its suggestions about policy were to be 'with full regard to the concept of education as a process continuing throughout life'. Lifelong learning by another name. As an aside, the significance of the elision from development to advisory as envisaged by Russell retrospectively proved to be ominous for what happened to the final ACACE report (ACACE 1982).

At the same time the Manpower Services Commission was created within the Employment Department. As the name implies, the Commission was charged with the task of finding effective ways of increasing the skill and knowledge base in all forms of employment to sustain the country's economic life in a healthy condition to cope with increasing international competition. It was funded by siphoning off monies which had supported further education. It became a strong development arm, influenced and controlled by central government, operating outside the sphere of local government. As such it marked the first significant step in reducing the scope of local authorities as providers of post-compulsory education. As the years went by and the MSC went through various permutations of nomenclature it became the government's front-line developer of vocational education and training at all levels. This was to be the future under successive Tory governments.

By the time the ACACE submitted what turned out to be its final report, a Tory government was in power. What Labour would have done in responding to that report is one of those unanswerable 'What if...' questions. As it was, the report got short shrift from the new government. Indeed Sir Keith Joseph sent a letter to Hoggart, saying that he would allow ACACE one more year, after which it would be closed down. There can be little doubt that the 'not one of us' factor got to work with a vengeance. Hoggart had to go as did much of his work as a staunch labour supporter, just as he was fired from the Arts Council as its Deputy Chairman.

By the time Richard Hoggart's final report from the ACACE was submitted in 1982, immediately before it was disbanded, the narrowing of what was known as adult education was there for everyone to see. The report produced incontrovertible evidence of a high demand – higher than expected – for what would be labelled 'informal learning' at a time when there were over a million students in formal adult education classes. It quoted many responses from the public which supported that old vision of Tawney. Individuals spoke of more education so as to be more 'whole', to 'understand better', to 'broaden' their minds. Referring to these responses in *An Imagined Life*, Richard Hoggart says, 'You wanted to throw your hat in the air' (Hoggart 1992: 214).

Exit ACACE

However, instead of responding positively to the recommendation that there should be a central body of some kind specially to promote and monitor continuing adult education, a development organisation, a recommendation that was costed, the Secretary of State not only rejected it but emasculated it by the Department's cherry-picking of its recommendations. Unlike Thatcher, Joseph did not shelve the report. He simply disbanded the Advisory Council which produced it and got rid of Hoggart into the bargain. Instead of taking the main thrust of that report seriously, he accepted a three-way split on adult learning devised by his senior civil servants.

The Department introduced something called 'the Unit for the Development of Adult and Continuing Education' and put it in the National Institute for Adult and Continuing Education to lift it out of its rather moribund condition, which at that point was concerned largely with university adult education. It was a soft money-driven project unit, fed regularly by funds from its parent, namely the government. It did valuable work in drawing attention to access problems for individuals seeking higher education, but, in retrospect, perhaps the most important initiative it took and probably the only one which continued into normal life was the earliest development of Open Colleges. It lasted until 1995 when it was amalgamated with the Further Education Development Agency, another body which arose from the ashes of dismantling, this time the Further Education Unit.

The second invention was something called 'Professional, industrial, commercial updating'. Again this was funded by the Department. The idea was to use project funds to persuade universities to develop schemes of skills and knowledge updating in collaboration with employers, for retraining in all those areas of economic activity which would boost the country's economic performance. Many institutions scrambled for the money but it is debatable how far-reaching were the effects, measured in productivity terms, which was what the government was after. It was probably more influential in producing some modest change of attitude than any long-term alteration in practice.

The third invention was the Return to Employment Plan (REPlan). As its name suggests this, the third government-funded new unit, was charged with finding ways of enabling the unemployed to become employed. As with PICKUP it had limited success, though as an initiative it was an important indication of government concern.

It is impossible to cost these three inventions, but it is a fair guess that, combined, they amounted to more than the central overarching unit that Hoggart had recommended. The obvious deduction is that through these three new units the Department of Education and Science kept an iron hand of control not only on funds but on policy development, and so of practice. Instead of Richard Hoggart and a posse of professionals riding off enthusiastically across the horizon with bright ideas by the score for the development of adult education in a liberal mould, the Secretary of State had a senior civil servant as Commissar of all three.

Vocational enshrined

It is difficult to exaggerate the long-term significance of that response to the final ACACE Report. All governments are driven to exert as much control as possible over everything. That is no surprise. What is more significant about Joseph's actions in relation to the current condition of lifelong learning is the strong nudge his threefold initiative gave towards the vocational. Two out of those initiatives had that explicit brief and the third was prompted by economic worries and widening participation for higher education. Two years later, in 1986, vocational learning was stamped on the country with the invention of the National Council for Vocational Qualifications (NCVQ). So in a sense the compass was set. The adult learning which was fundable was vocational learning, and, as the intended chief developer, further education found its funding tied increasingly to vocational outputs.

And so did local authorities. The Higher and Further Education Act of 1992 repeated that 'It shall be the duty of every local education authority to secure provision for their area of adequate facilities for further education', but it altered the funding system to support that duty. That duty did not apply to what was known as Schedule 2, namely courses which did not lead to formal qualifications. LEAs were left to support non-vocational activities at their discretion. It was another tilt towards vocational education and training as the predominating influence in adult education, and hence another step in the evolution of the practice of lifelong learning. Churchill may have felt betrayed.

This is not to say that nothing needed to be done urgently about the bewildering number and range of occupational courses being offered by a plethora of examining bodies for hundreds of qualifications and so offered by colleges of further education. It was a pressing problem, particularly at a time when the government was panicky about the economy. The Department of Employment set up a Task Force to produce a scheme for rationalising and simplifying the whole range of vocational courses.

The National Council for Vocational Qualifications

The National Council for Vocational Qualifications was established in 1986 to do the job. It set about it by separating learning from assessment. It was not concerned with educational matters of curriculum and teaching. It was interested solely in whether or not an individual could meet the criteria for one of its competences. It recruited groups of employers to produce a hierarchy of competences for every conceivable occupation against which assessments would be made and graded towards the newly established National Vocational Qualifications (NVQ). All the existing examining bodies were invited to submit their courses for accreditation provided learning objectives were attached to each course and that they could demonstrate an equivalence with the necessary competences. All students following such courses were to be assessed against those competences and, if successful, they would be awarded the appropriate NVQ.

Huge amounts of money were invested in the NCVQ. Its brief was expanded from the purely vocational to qualifications known as General National Vocational Qualifications (GNVQs). This was an attempt to broaden the participation from those studying on regular vocational courses and the employed and unemployed to those in further education and secondary schools who were pursuing their general education. The idea was to build in some occupational competences to that general education as a supplement to their academic courses. This was another version of the long-standing attempt to increase the standing of occupational courses. It was part of a wider problem of trying to establish vocational courses at all levels as having the same reputation in the public mind as academic courses, and to somehow drag the vocational courses up to their level.

NCVQ had a relatively short life. It had limited success. Procedures proved too expensive. Philosophically and practically it trapped itself in a never-ending need to reformulate competences because in such a fast-changing world today's competences could be tomorrow's incompetences. The response from employers was nowhere near as enthusiastic as the NCVQ had assumed. Many further education colleges found the procedures too bureaucratic and expensive, but, most serious of all, it never reached the numbers of participants expected. It was scrapped in 2000 and amalgamated with yet another newly invented body, the Qualifications and Assessment Agency, where competences survive but under quite different regimes. But for fifteen years it promoted a particular form of

adult learning which was light years away from a balanced version of lifelong learning.

Thus by the mid-1980s the vocational was king in adult learning. The
argument which raged in the background about 'useful learning' or 'relevant learning' to differentiate vocational learning from learning undertaken for intellectual, social or other reasons seemed to have been won by
the 'useful' brigade. And it was king in a society where education had
been infected by managerial jargon so that the world of students and
learners became peopled with consumers, clients or customers. People
became counters for achieving targets as if education institutions were like
business and industry. Success equalled the number of qualifications
achieved. It was rampant instrumentalism. It was the Tories' application of
market economy principles but within a flawed market economy rigged by
the government. The reasoning was along the lines of assuming that
investment in training was investment in human capital, and was the
equivalent to capital investment in machinery in the nineteenth century.
The vocational's reign was relatively undisturbed until the beginnings of
ambivalence crept into the renamed Department for Education and
Employment from about 1998.

The vocational questioned

Meanwhile, the economic imperative behind vocational learning was
pursued by the Royal Society of Arts. Funded heavily first by the Department of Employment and the new DfEE, Sir Christopher Ball ran a series
of projects which produced reports with the titles of *Learning Pays* in 1991
and *Learning is Profitable* in 1992. These reports and the thinking behind
them produced a powerful counter-blast in the RSA's Edmund Rich
Memorial Lecture in 1995 given by Richard Smethurst, Provost of Worces-
ter College, Oxford, formerly a successor of Frank Jessup at the renamed
Oxford Department of External Studies, and Deputy Chairman of the
Monopolies and Mergers Committee. He had also served on Hoggart's
ACACE Committee. Smethurst called his lecture 'Education: a public or
private good?' During a long exploration of the ins and outs of the theory
of human capital in relation to investment in education he admitted that
he had changed his mind about the validity of any attempts to make any
explicit, detailed, causal connections between investment in education
and economic growth. He argued that the human capital approach to
adult learning was leading to a serious distortion in the emerging patterns
of provision for lifelong learning. He ended:

> Damage is being done; and what better body than ... the RSA to seek
> to limit it. Could it make a start by conceding that its own titles are too
> limited for a learning society; that its slogan should be not that learn-

ing is profitable, nor even that learning pays, but that learning, all learning ... any learning in higher education, further education, secondary and primary and nursery education, professional development courses, the WEA, the NFWI, countless voluntary groups and societies (remember how many ACACE found in the voluntary sector in its North West Study (in the Hoggart Report)) ... that all learning is valuable.

(Smethurst 1995)

This dispute surfaced again in 1999 at the RSA during a debate on 'Our learning society' between Sir Christopher Ball and Professor Coffield who had conducted a major research project on 'The learning society' funded by the Social Science Research Committee.
  Sir Christopher Ball laid out his position:

My thesis is that the challenge of learning lies more in the realm of motivation than of provisions and that market forces are better suited than public services than solving the problem.

Professor Coffield's position was different:

Sir Christopher emphasises an individual approach to learning whereas I argue for the importance of social structure. Surveys show that about 30 per cent of the adult population are not participating in any kind of formal training or learning and that non-participants come predominately from social classes IV and V. Non participation is not a personal trouble but a public issue which requires public response at the level of policy.

(Ball and Coffield 1999)

This seemed to be a variation on the vocational versus liberal purpose of continuing learning: useless versus useful learning. Market forces as a motive connect easily with economic purposes of lifelong learning whereas social structure is implying a far wider concern than the economic. It is worth noting in passing that Coffield placed strong emphasis on 'formal training or learning'. It was at this conference that Professor Bob Fryer, Chair of the government's Task Force on lifelong learning, observed:

There is a presupposition that we know what a learning society looks like. We need more debate on what we mean by it and why we want it, and that will make us challenge many of the ways we do things at the moment.

For all the chat there is little evidence that things are being done differently. Fryer might well ask if there is any evidence, and if there is not, why not?

However, in the mid-1990s the emphasis was so heavily on the economically driven vocational version of lifelong learning that the difficulties were laid bare of getting a hearing for what can still be called the liberal education version of lifelong learning as pronounced by Smethurst. And in many ways it is a sterile argument. The idea that the two versions of lifelong learning cannot accommodate one another is plain rubbish. It was rubbish however that had to be cleared away to make way for a more satisfying understanding of what lifelong learning means for people, whether or not they are engaged in contributing directly to the economy through work.

Government as promoter of lifelong learning

When the Labour government was elected in May 1997 it inherited the Kennedy Committee and received its report in June (DfEE 1997b).This had a lot to say about lifelong learning and undoubtedly served to move the topic up the political and education agenda. It also inherited the Dearing Committee of Inquiry into Higher Education which issued its report in July 1997 just two months after Labour had taken office. This Report was entitled *Higher Education in the Learning Society* (DfEE 1997a). As the name implies, like the Kennedy Report it had a good deal to say about lifelong learning and complemented Kennedy's coverage of further education by adding higher education, and so encompassed most of post-secondary education. As such it laid more emphasis again on the reasons for increasing lifelong learning and so highlighted its importance. Something of a climatic change was occurring, but only on one part of the horizon.

Dearing saw a learning society 'in which people in all walks of life recognise the need to continue in education and learning throughout their working lives and who see learning as enhancing the quality of life throughout its stages' (DfEE 1997a: 9). Decoded, this means again seeing individuals and their working lives sustaining a competitive economy. Since both Kennedy and Dearing talk about a return to learning as if formal learning was the only kind of learning worth mentioning, large stretches of the horizon remain unchanged in these two documents.

The government itself lost no time in saying something about lifelong learning. Whether it was influenced by this OECD statement in 1995 cannot be known. The Secretary General issued 'Making life long learning a reality for all' in which the following appeared:

> Continuing to expand education and training systems that rely upon learning opportunities limited to early life – 'more of the same' – will

not suffice as a strategy for meeting today's challenges.... Much has been said over the years about lifelong learning but, in truth, it is still a reality only for a tiny segment of the populations of the OECD countries. The huge task now facing OECD Governments is to make it a reality for a progressively expanding part of the population so that it eventually becomes a reality for all.

This was a resounding ring of the obvious, but if it served to tickle the government's fancy just a little then it was worth issuing.

Subsequently, Jacques Delors had this to say in 1996:

There is a need to rethink and broaden the notion of lifelong education. Not only must it adapt itself to changes in the nature of work, but it must also constitute a continuous process of forming whole human beings – their knowledge and aptitudes, as well as the critical faculty and ability to act. It should enable people to develop awareness of themselves and their environment and encourage them to play their social role at work and in the community.

(Fryer 1997)

This harks back to the inspired purposes of adult education envisaged by Tawney and Mansberg. In effect it says that economics are not enough. Churchill would have approved. Thus concern about what lifelong learning was for was in the air.

It is always impossible to attribute a causal connection between public statements about policy and government's shifting interpretations of its own policy statements. The Russell Report is a good example of how influence can affect future events. However, wherever that influence came from there was *Learning for the Twenty First Century*, the first report of the National Advisory Group for Continuing Education and Lifelong Learning, and the Fryer Report, which the Secretary of State commissioned to give advice for the formulation of the imminent White Paper on Education (Fryer 1997). So change was in the air in what had become the Department for Education and Employment. It is perhaps interestingly coincidental that by February 1998 some widening of the purposes of lifelong learning found their way into the DfEE's Green Paper *The Learning Age: A New Renaissance for a New Britain* (DfEE 1998a), and its statements and examples in its prospectus for the Adult and Community Learning Fund. *The Learning Age* was issued with what can be fairly described as an almost visionary commitment by the Secretary of State David Blunkett in his Introduction.

As well as securing our economic future, learning has a wider contribution. It helps make ours a civilised society, develops the spiritual side of our lives and promotes active citizenship. Learning enables people to play a full part in their community. It strengthens the family, the neighbourhood and consequently the nation. It helps us fulfil our potential and opens doors to a love of music, art and literature. That is why we value learning for its own sake as well as for the equality of opportunity it brings.

Earlier, *Learning and Working Together for the Future* was published as a consultation document by the DfEE (DfEE 1997c). It listed seven what it called key challenges. One was 'To make a reality of lifelong learning' and another was 'Tackling depravation and social exclusion'. Raising standards, moving people from welfare into work, a fair labour market and partnerships were among the others.

The section on lifelong learning leans heavily on training deficiencies, the need for skill enhancement and so the need for greater investment from employers. The section on social exclusion is more concerned with people as people, and talks glowingly about tackling deprivation in all the many ways which are disfiguring society.

The 1998 version, *Learning and Working Together for the Future: A Strategic Framework to 2002* (DfEE 1998b), sharpens the focus even-handedly. One of the two challenges it cites under the heading 'To work with others across government' is 'To create an inclusive society'. The other is 'To build an internationally competitive economy'. One of the DfEE's objectives is 'To develop in everyone a commitment to lifelong learning'. This is expanded on the next page as 'To develop in everyone a commitment to lifelong learning, so as to enhance their lives, improve their employability in a changing labour market and create the skills that our economy and employers need'. The other two are to do with enabling young people to be well equipped to deal with the world as they find it and to help people get work. Again the section on social exclusion is eloquent but tends to veer into the economic reasons for seeking improvement. All this leads to a brief commentary on economic and technical change and globalisation which precedes this ringing commitment, and needs to be quoted in full.

> Together these trends pose **two major challenges**: to create a society that is inclusive and an economy which can compete in the global market place.
>
> Learning is of particular importance to the **socially excluded** who suffer from some or all of a lack of skills, no work, low esteem, low expectations, fragmented communities, poor housing, crime, ill-health and drugs: problems which have often persisted over several generations. The challenge for the DfEE is to re-engage individuals in developing their skills – to reduce the numbers of children excluded from schools or playing truant; raise achievement in schools so that

young people continue in education and training; encourage young people or adults who were failed by their schools to get back into learning; help those without jobs to find ways back to work and to promote equality of opportunity and outcome for people across all sections of society.

An internationally competitive economy requires firms that are agile, with the skills and enterprise to create and sustain competitive advantage. This means Government fostering an environment which supports and stimulates that agility through economic policies that provide stability, not boom and bust, and that can handle external shocks. The challenge for the DfEE is to work with employers and education and training providers to ensure that young people and adults are equipped for tomorrow – with the skills, attitudes and personal qualities that will match the changing jobs, and are able to enhance and update their skills as requirements intensify.

Meeting these challenges demands joined-up government – close collaboration with Government Offices in the regions, the Social Exclusion Unit and Departments such as the Department of Trade and Industry, Department of Social Security, the Treasury, Department for Environment, Transport and the Regions, Department of Health and the Home Office. It also demands active Government support for strong local partnerships that will knit together national policies and programmes to deliver results on the ground.

In the light of these two challenges the DfEE has revised its Department aims as follows:

To give everyone the chance, through education, training and work, to realise their full potential, and thus build an inclusive and fair society and a competitive economy.

To support this aim the DfEE has also set itself three specific objectives:

1   To ensure that all young people reach 16 with the skills, attitudes and personal qualities that will give them a secure foundation for lifelong learning, work and citizenship in a rapidly changing world.
2   To develop in everyone a commitment to lifelong learning, so as to enhance their lives, improve their employability in a changing labour market and create the skills that our economy and employers need.

The basis for lifelong learning – enthusiasm for self development – has to be laid down in schools, with careers education helping individuals to make the link between self development and achievement and all our people encouraged to continue in education or training after 16, complete their courses and achieve further qualifications.

But to establish the habit of lifelong learning amongst adults we have to:

- encourage broader programmes of education and training for 16–19 year olds, including development of key skills;
- have active policies to persuade those whose schooling was not a success to re-engage with learning;
- encourage individuals to invest in their own development;
- offer them better information, advice and guidance throughout life about the skills that will increase their employability;
- make learning more accessible;
- have credible qualifications that allow them to demonstrate their growing skills;
- promote high quality and standards in universities and colleges;
- get those providing education and training to be more responsive to individuals' needs, and to widen access;
- persuade employers to invest in the skills of all those they employ.

3   To help people without a job into work.

This wide-ranging commitment to lifelong learning runs through the Department's *Adult and Community Learning Fund Prospectus* also published in 1998. It follows on from the *Learning Age* and, although it does not use the words 'lifelong learning', that is what it is all about. Tessa Blackstone's Introduction about learning being at the heart of the government's ambitions begins with what could be taken as a ringing endorsement of Churchill's views all those years ago:

It helps to make ours a civilised society, develops the spiritual side to our lives and promotes active citizenship. Learning enables people to play a full part in their community. It strengthens the family, the neighbourhood and consequently the nation.

As a direct quote from Blunkett's Introduction to the 1998 Green Paper, it is evidence that the wider view of lifelong learning was present and correct. True, there is the usual reference to people needing the basic skills but without explicit reference to the economy: 'People who find it difficult to make the English language work for them have less chance of dealing effectively with all aspects of our modern information-rich society.'

The list of activities which were eligible for financial support from the Fund are indeed community-based. The document shows a welcome understanding that to improve basic skills it is not necessary and probably ineffective to mount a frontal attack. Support for debt counselling, school managers, health visitors, CAB volunteers, rural support groups, offenders in motor vehicle crime, resettlement services for the homeless, estate management for tenants' associations, personal financial management skills for single parents, all feature in the list of possibilities. Some refer to basic skills acquisition, but not all. It is an impressively imaginative series of suggestions as how to engage with adults as learners right across the board. Placed alongside the government's promotion of Healthy Living Centres, Employment Action Teams and New Deal for Communities, all of which incidentally rely heavily on voluntary bodies, there is solid evidence that important shifts were taking place in the content of what could be called lifelong learning.

The government-funded RSA's Project 2001 mounted in collaboration with the Voluntary Sector National Training Organisation and the National Training Organisation for Arts Entertainment and Cultural Heritage was in the same spirit. The idea was to try to exploit the opportunities for learning in voluntary organisations. By offering accreditation for what they could do and know, volunteers in some 200 organisations were helped to formulate plans for improving their performance and then putting those plans into action. This represented a large-scale application of the assessment of prior experiential learning. Simultaneously the project produced solid evidence of the potential of voluntary organisations as places of learning and thus of how they can contribute to the overall development of lifelong learning.

It was almost as if the government had caught up with voluntary organisations. Every item on that list of commitments could be shown to be undertaken by one or other voluntary body, and had been done for a long time. Thus, having got way out of step with an inclusive, humane, all-embracing understanding of what lifelong learning meant for ordinary people, the government seemed to have mended its ways and fallen back into line. The New Labour government set a different course. It was applying common sense. The thinking was there about the purposes, ways and means of developing lifelong learning. The problem was, and is, implementation.

But then comes the Foundation degree proposal with its heavy emphasis on vocational preparation, sponsorship by and involvement with employers. Quite apart from the awkward question about where students are going to come from to enrol on a two-year programme which is of the same standard as a three-year degree course, there is the haunting suspicion that it is a variation of the succession of schemes designed over the past twenty-five years to upgrade the skills and knowledge of the working population. It is almost as if vocational learning was not content with what was said about it in *Learning and Working Together for the Future* but insisted on having something specific. This emerged as a demand for enhancing the vocational capabilities of those sections of the population who were not already engaged in higher education by enrolling them on specifically work-related studies as deliberate vocational preparation. It was as if it had to be shouted loud and clear to counteract the broader vision that the Secretary of State propounded in the earlier document. The difficulties of getting the right balance within lifelong learning between 'useful' and/or pleasure learning had not gone away.

This was a little odd, since there had been plenty of youth training schemes, none of which ever showed more than a very modest success, largely because the training was for jobs which did not exist. There was the Open Tec, supposedly a white-hot technological exploitation of information technology, to make available a wide range of training programmes to individual companies, and it was hoped, through them, to their employees. This was followed by the Open College which attempted to do the same thing, but through printed versions of programmes which were either home-grown or bought in from other providers. Then came the National Council for Vocational Qualifications, with its attempt to turn training on its head so that it was the learners' interest which came first rather than the people and institutions who provided training programmes. The idea was to uncouple learning from assessment so that whether anything was learned mattered not; the only question to be answered was whether a man or woman did or did not have a particular competence. A small number of education ideologues pushed this idea to its limit so that almost every employment activity of the land had its operation described in ascending hierarchies of competence. Historians will later be able to assess the worthwhileness of this initiative compared with the huge sums of public money invested in it. It was an attempt to tie additional learning for adults to immediate economic effectiveness. It was lifelong learning for vocational enhancement.

There were also the Training and Enterprise Councils (TECs) in the late 1980s. At the time many said that they represented the last chance for employers to avoid legal compulsion, to become serious contributors to employee development because, if they failed, the next stop was enforcement through legislation. In the event nothing so dramatic has occurred. Like all the other attempts to beef up training and skills enhancement they had limited success, but in many ways they were different from previous initiatives. Each of the eighty-two TECs was created as a limited company with a board composed of a majority of employers with some educators and a token representation from local authorities from which they were completely separate. Their brief was to develop economic activity in all ways possible for its area. They were inhibited, some would say prevented, from doing their job by Treasury regulations which controlled finances. An annual budgeting procedure made it well-nigh impossible to lay long-term plans, but a more fundamental reason for their limited performance was a lack of motivation on all sides. Employers found the annual budgeting intolerable – their firms would go bankrupt under any such system. Local authorities were deliberately sidelined so they had no incentive to become vigorous promoters. And since, as everyone agreed, the main problem about retraining and updating lay with small and medium-sized companies, the absence of a consistent system of financial support with clear strategies for engaging SMEs meant that the entire business was a hit-and-miss affair.

It was hardly surprising then that the Labour government of 1997 determined to review TECs and replace them with something calculated to be more effective. So the TECs were scrapped. The National Learning and Skills Council was subsequently created, and to promote and oversee its activities it has forty-seven regional skills councils. As if to underline the point, the Department for Education and Employment was renamed the Department for Education and Skills.

The omens for the National Learning and Skills Council (LSC) are different from its predecessors and, if it can stick to its brief, rather more encouraging, too. As a national body with forty-seven regional councils as its prime operational arm its purpose as stated by its Chief Executive is to change the level of skills and knowledge in the country. There is nothing new there worth lingering on, but it is committed to a fourfold developmental programme. It is charged to get more young people engaged as participant learners beyond the school-leaving age. Of course it is expected to provide an economic boost. Similarly it is no surprise to find that raising standards is its third charge, but then comes the new and radical element in government policy about encouraging learning. The LSC has a statutory requirement to increase participation and stimulate it.

Its task is huge. It inherits responsibility financially for all the previous work done by the Further Education Funding Council, the funding of adult education, sixth-form colleges, all the youth schemes and the schemes run by local authorities themselves. It means coping with all post-secondary education apart from higher education. If it is to succeed then it will need to treat the world of voluntary organisations in the same way as it treats statutory organisations. It cannot do its job without them. That of itself is an important shift in the official conception of lifelong learning. The Chief Executive committed the LSC publicly to just that in a speech in the British Library on 8 March 2001 to the final conference of the RSA's project: 'Learning and skills in the voluntary sector: priorities for action'.

One aspect of the LSC will help it to do its job. It is a national body with a national remit. Unlike the TECs which were without any national development body and so went their eighty-seven different ways, the LSC can act as a cohering influence if it chooses to do so. As such it has the capacity, on paper at any rate, of striking a better balance between the skills and learning sides of its title than has been seen for twenty-five years; indeed since from the time when the government became concerned about the level of skills required to keep the economy healthy. This possibility is strengthened by one of the terms of the Learning and Skills Act of 2000 which said that the separation of Schedule I courses from Schedule 2 was scrapped. So whereas that separation had forbidden local authorities to support financially courses or classes which did not lead to formal qualifications, the new act empowers them to support both award-bearing and non-award-bearing provision. This applies to voluntary bodies as well.

Individual learning accounts

This seemed set fair to become even more important when set alongside individual learning accounts, another initiative introduced by David Blunkett when he was Secretary of State (DfEE 1998c). Alas, that all went wrong. Thirteen months after they were introduced, Estelle Morris, Blunkett's successor as Secretary of State, closed down the programme. Sloppy financial management led to accusations of fraudulent use of public funds, and an unseemly difference of opinion developed between the main contractor for the scheme and the DfES as to who was responsible for the poor financial supervision which made possible the misuse of taxpayers' money.

What is so galling about that failure is that it need not have happened. It is an elementary requirement to avoid financial problems. But it was flawed from the outset. In a seminar at the London Institute of Education in 2000 Professor David Robertson warned that in applying the idea of individual learning accounts to the lower end of the training spectrum it was courting disaster. Better, he said, to begin such a new initiative at the higher education end of the spectrum where monitoring would be relatively easy and success more or less guaranteed because of clear criteria for eligibility. On the basis of proven success he claimed, with some confidence, that it would be possible to expand the range of education and training activities which could be covered by individual learning accounts.

As well as galling, the failure of individual learning accounts struck a devastating blow to the ideas for expanding lifelong learning. It was one of the few genuinely innovative schemes to promoting it. A chance was missed, a chance which ought to have been a shot in the arm both for providers and potential learners. There is nothing like a possible financial benefit to tickle motivation.

Things were coming full circle. Lifelong learning had moved from learning for its own sake through a succession of permutations of vocational initiatives, each of which was intended somehow to boost the economy, and now back to the 'level playing field' basis for funding through the LSC both of vocational and non-vocational learning as offered by voluntary bodies as well as by formal education institutions.

Lifelong learning may begin to look rather different. The LSC seems a natural expression operationally not only of the spirit but the detail in *Learning and Working Together for the Future.*

Trade unions

Individual learning accounts is a good point to refer to the trade union contributions to an evolving sense of lifelong learning and its practice because of the union learning representatives which emerged as a parallel government initiative. Ever since their beginning, trade unions have been concerned to promote education and training as a means of improving the circumstances of their members and have always had some educational and training programmes as part of their service to their members. Some unions have highly developed education departments with premises to match. Until fairly recently Ruskin College at Oxford was the most frequently used route towards further study and higher education qualifications as unions sponsored members so that they could attend that college. Now there are other routes open for educational advancement. Courses have been developed in partnership with universities and colleges. Connections with the WEA were close, and after the Second World War, interest quickened in individual trade unions in providing education programmes themselves.

Individual unions such as the General and Municipal Workers, the Transport and General Workers and the Amalgamated Engineering Union all offered short courses to their members on topics such as work study, industrial relations, methods of payment, factory organisation and production control. In 1957 the TUC set up a Training College and Department of Educations were created in many unions. By 1960 some 15,000 students were enrolled on weekend and short courses offered by the National Council for Labour Colleges. By 1968 there were some 24,000 enrolled on TUC schemes (Holford 1994), but unions generally kept their own education and training to themselves and were not related closely to formal education systems, although there were close links with Ruskin College and the Northern Men's College.

Once APEL was a going concern during the 1980s and 1990s there were many approaches to individual unions to try to persuade their members of its potential value. The GMB and the AEU, later Unison, listened politely, sometimes even sounding as if they would take it up. Disappointingly no one did. This was puzzling, particularly at a time when unions were losing members partially due to the impact of Tory legislation and monetary policies. APEL could have been used as a recruiting device, an additional service for members. It would have been lifelong learning in a different context.

More recently the developments promoted by the Union Learning

Fund (ULF) established by government in 1998 (DfEE 1998d) seek specifically to enlist unions so as to take education into places not reached hitherto. Within trade unions lifelong learning took on a different role. In the DfEE document *The Learning Age* (DfEE 1998a), there was reference to union learning representatives (ULRs). By 2002 3,500 voluntary ULRs had been trained and the intention was to raise that number to 22,000 by 2012. The claim was that this number would mean that about half a million trade union members would be serviced by the ULRs. The scheme has statutory backing in the Employment Relations Bill. The training courses for volunteers are accredited by the Open College Network.

This becomes more impressive when the roles of the ULRs are set out. They are expected to analyse the learning and training needs of individuals. They provide information and advice on learning opportunities. They arrange for learning and training opportunities to be provided. They promote ideas about the value of learning. They consult with employers about doing all this with union representatives.

They do it all as volunteers. Some are shop stewards but many are those who up until now had not been active members, but have seized on the range of activities offered in becoming an ULR as something which enriches their lives. Many testify to this, as do those who have been helped by a ULR.

Employers support the scheme. They say that it helps develop a sense of team work, that it builds up the confidence of employees, that it improves employees' skills and productivity, and above all it promotes better industrial relations. According to York Consulting who conducted an evaluation of the scheme, it cost the employers between 7.5 and 10 days of an employee's time to fulfil the role of a ULR (TUC 2002).

The Public and Commercial Service Union (PCS) has shown how the ULR scheme can be deployed within a government agency: the Inland Revenue. In 'Our time' this appears as a comment on an arrangement organised jointly by the Inland Revenue, the PCS and the TUC.

> This is the first time that management and PCS have worked together where it has clearly worked. PCS members have benefited from being able to use learn direct courses in work time free of charge.
>
> (PCS 2002)

There are a host of enthusiastic reports from bakers, engineers, shop workers, textile workers, co-op workers, and metroline bus and train drivers (TUC 2002a). Many claim that 'it changed the way they saw things'.

So this appears to be a government initiative which is not only working well, engaging additional groups of people in LLL, but is full of possibilities for further development. More of that later.

The voluntaries

So if the government seems to have realigned itself with those who have been working with the sort of lifelong learning that it now seeks to promote, it has to be set against the way that, during this period the evolution of lifelong learning moved from being a relatively small-scale enterprise for people who just wanted to know more about the world they lived in, to government efforts to promote it as a large-scale enterprise but essentially to contribute to strengthening the economy and now back again. Meanwhile in the background and rarely brought to the public's attention, many voluntary organisations continued to quietly expand and develop their own contributions to lifelong learning. It is important to place them on record as vital influences on the evolving meaning of lifelong learning.

On the borderline between formal and informal provision for adults to learn more, there are the Open College networks. Open Colleges as a new phenomenon began in the late 1980s, then the Unit for the Development of Adult and Community Education spent much of its early effort investigating ways of overcoming obstacles which deterred people from seeking access to higher education. During those discussions, David Browing had the idea of trying to find ways of enticing adults to learn more when it was perfectly clear that they would go nowhere near a formal college of any kind. Through him the first Open College opened in Manchester, tackling the tricky questions of accreditation, acceptability and thus progression leading to access.

There are now some twenty-nine local Open College networks (OCNs) covering England, Wales and Northern Ireland. Local OCNs make up the National Open College Network (NOCN) on a membership basis. Local OCNs comprise FE colleges, voluntary organisations, HEIs, LEAs and membership organisations. The majority are companies limited by guarantee and registered charities. They operate under licence from the National Open College Network which in turn is approved by the Qualifications and Curriculum Agency as a national qualifications-awarding body under QCA regulations. The NOCN approves accreditation procedures, on a unitised basis, for further education and adult education. No less important, its programmes range from one credit at Entry Level for basic skills up to Level 3 access programmes. This is a serious, significant addition to possibilities for informal and formal learning because the NOCN is a national awarding body, like EdExcel, and the Royal Society of Arts. None of this existed before APEL came on the scene, and it was APEL which first sparked interest in providing opportunities through OCNs for people who went nowhere near a further education college.

Moreover, the range of the curriculum has been expanded and codified since its early beginnings. The Annual Review for 2000 lists activities under access to higher education, working with communities, family learning, basic skills, work-based learning, working with colleges, working with voluntary organisations and working with young people. It shows that the numbers of people joining OCN activities have risen by 13 per cent between 1998 and 1999/2000, and during the same period those seeking credit for their learning achievements has risen by 22 per cent.

This all flies under the original banner of Social Exclusion. As the Annual Report puts it: 'Widening participation and tackling social exclusion have risen to the top of the political agenda, alongside a raft of policies and initiatives designed to raise standards and achievement.' The NOCN is doing its bit. For the year 1999 to 2000 learner registrations were 663,000. That is a very large number of adults who wish to return to learning voluntarily and, whatever their reasons for doing so, it is solely because they want to. As an indication of how far the story of the evolution of lifelong learning has come in 2001 it is hugely significant.

The WEA has been mentioned already. Its part in the story is different and of course it pre-dates Open Colleges by the best part of a century. Its current story continues to be a convincing and innovative example of lifelong learning. Its annual report shows that for the year ending July 2000, nationally there were 130,000 students enrolled and 10,000 courses provided. Over the past decade the WEA has exceeded the target numbers on which its subventions from public funds are based. It has sixteen district offices. Its activities are grouped under three headings: General programme; Community learning programme and Workplace learning programme. The first is a continuation of its long-standing tradition of classes in the humanities, local history and the social sciences, with an accurate reflection of the expanding interests of so many people; the history of furniture, the environment, rock climbing, abstract art are just some examples. This remains the largest element in the overall national programme. The next largest part of the programme is the community programme which is aimed at groups with particular needs and invariably are offered in partnership with other organisations. Overall, as its name suggests, it is concerned primarily with widening participation and social inclusion. This is an important point to register for the WEA. Basic skills would have looked entirely out of place in the programmes of the pre- and early postwar periods. Now it appears in pride of place alongside helping in schools, women and health, and work with refugees and ethnic minorities. The Workplace learning programme focuses particularly on lower paid workers and is run in collaboration with a number of trades unions: Unison, GMB and MSF. Its partnership with the Open College Network makes it the largest provider using the NOCN and it works with the Open University to open up additional progression routes for members to move on to further and higher education.

So the WEA has kept up with the changes to society going on around it. As the lines between the so-called working class and middle class have become progressively blurred and the economic and social structure of the country has changed, so has the range of courses expanded, as is indicated by the threefold division of its provision. A central part of its work concerns social inclusion as it always has. The way it meets the contemporary nature of exclusion focuses on a different range of social contexts from those which were the concern if its founders; that concern remains predominate. But as a prime vehicle for the development of lifelong learning it has few peers. Its story offers lessons for others to learn about how best to tackle it for many constituencies.

This is seen clearly in the introduction to the Annual Report for the South Eastern District, 2000/2001, which claims the WEA's uniqueness is based on a combination of elements. It:

- is committed to taking learning opportunities to the learner;
- has particular commitment to the needs of those who missed out on learning in earlier life;
- involves its learners in decisions about their learning both individually and collectively;
- is managed democratically by its members and learners;
- works in partnership with many other organisations to meet learning needs;
- seeks to offer good-quality learning experiences underpinned by effective tutor training and support as well as regular monitoring and evaluation.

This reads like a brief for one of the Secretary of State's clarion calls for lifelong learning.

Not everyone would assume that the Citizens Advice Bureau (CAB) is involved with lifelong learning. Its advice and support role in countless towns is greatly valued. Indeed it is part of the social structure which keeps life moving for many. Its first aim is 'to ensure that individuals do not suffer through lack of knowledge about their rights and responsibilities or of the services available to help them, or through an inability to express their needs effectively' It provides for all that through the 2,000 or so bureaux, each of which is a registered charity and linked to the National Association of Citizens Advice Bureau. Tacitly that is a version of lifelong learning, from helping people to understand where they stand in relation to various statutory entitlements or to find their way around the bureaucracies concerned with housing and social services, to essentially helping them to learn more about the circumstances of their own lives. To do that, its Annual Report shows that there are 23,000 volunteers serving in the 2,000 bureaux, of which 12,503 are advisers, 7,342 are management committee members and the remaining 3,000-plus serve in other roles. It is reasonable to assume that a fair proportion of those 23,000 are learning all the time as they try to keep abreast of changing regulations for social services and housing benefits and so on. It would not be called LLL of course, but for those members of the general public whom they seek to serve, tacitly it is just that: a version of lifelong learning.

None of this is surprising, except perhaps for the scale of the CAB operation when set down in black and white, but to see it as a specific lifelong learning provider is not necessarily expected. In the text of the Annual Report for 1999/2000 which describes how it tries to fulfil that aim it includes training as part of the way it attends to standards so that its volunteers are able to serve effectively in CAB outlets. For any one year it offers 4,500 places on training courses in six different locations. In the year ending 2000, some new 4,000 volunteers took up places. These training courses are thoroughgoing educational programmes.

However, these training programmes serve other purposes besides ensuring that volunteers are equipped to do the job in a CAB. They are formally accredited to the National Open College Network. This means that the CAB has put itself on a ladder of learning opportunities which is open to all its volunteers who have completed the training course to use for whatever purpose they wish. It might be the satisfaction of having learning achievements recognised officially, or it might be a step on the route to further qualifications through cashing in the OCN credits awarded.

The CAB is developing its role as a training and learning provider further. In collaboration with the University of Staffordshire, it is developing a distance learning package in advice studies. The intention is to provide a structure which enables CAB volunteers as students to move through the three ascending levels of study: certificate, diploma and then degree studies. It is seeking formal recognition from the Qualifications and Curriculum Agency for designating its training and education programmes as a National Qualification in Advice Studies.

Nor is that all. Given the substantial nature of the training programme it is hardly surprising to find that some 38 per cent of the trained volunteers move on to employment. The background to this is that volunteers are recruited from three broad categories: the under-25s, women under the inelegant label 'women returners', and the early retired. It means however that in order to ensure that its own services are up to standard the CAB is providing opportunities not only for its volunteers to move along the qualification route, but as a proving ground for those who decide that they want paid employment. If that is not lifelong learning it is hard to think what it can be.

Then there is the National Trust. Everyone knows about it. Even so its scale is something of a surprise when put into words. It has 2,643,173 members. It has 38,000 volunteers. But not everyone realises that it is a significant actor on the adult learning scene. In the latest Annual Report

(2000/2001) this appears: 'making education and lifelong learning integral to everything we do.' It claims that this is one of the ways it seeks to show how the Trust is 'making a real difference to the quality of life of people in this country'. And anyone who visits one of the Trust's properties gets a flavour of that. History speaks directly as buildings, furniture, pictures and *objets d'art* engage the attention of visitors, with carefully written commentaries on what can be seen. Opportunities for learning are provided more deliberately when demonstrations are mounted of cooking, using recipes, utensils and stoves as authentic accounts of how things were done in the past. Or methods of farming or woodland management are sometimes displayed through various forms of demonstration.

What may be a surprise to some is that there is a section in the Trust's Annual Report entitled 'Extending adult education'. In some houses visitors are invited to use some of the materials on hand and try their hands at painting what they see in gardens, advised by professional artists. In association with the WEA it runs courses. A series of study days are arranged from the identification of fungi to what is listed as 'putting a house to bed'. Residential bird-watching, sailing, painting and cookery courses are part of its programme, as are what are called 'family fun weekends' available to adults at the Brancaster Millennium Activity Centre in Norfolk. And there is the training of volunteers. As well as an induction programme there are courses on conservation, security and presentation, health and safety, managing and developing other volunteers, and public facing roles.

The list of voluntary organisations which are involved in one way or another with lifelong learning goes on. Like the National Trust and the Citizens Advice Bureau, the Women's Institute is a huge organisation which reaches into every corner of the country. For the year 2000 the National Federation of Women's Institutes (NFWI) recorded that there were 240,000 members in 7,500 WIs organised in seventy county and island federations. The NFWI Millennium Survey based on a representative sample of one in ten local WIs shows an interesting pattern of growth and development. Some 34 per cent of these WIs were formed before 1930 with the number of newly formed WIs tailing off to 21 per cent between 1996 and 2000. They are not small: some 67 per cent comprise between twenty-one and fifty members.

There are two other factors which the Millennium Survey records and which connect with the LLL part of the story. One is the age of WI members. What is particularly interesting here is to see those ages against demography. Whereas only 7 per cent of those members were under the age of 40, some 14 per cent were aged between 41 and 50, rising to 24 per cent for those aged 51 to 60, rising again to 30 per cent for the 61- to 70-year-olds and dropping to 24 per cent for the over-seventies.

The second item in the survey which is of particular interest are the answers which WI members gave to questions about their awareness of the learning opportunities the WI offered and the kinds of topics they might like to take part in. The survey asked respondents to list in priority their choices from among the following list: Denman College, trustee training, art and craft, public affairs, travelling tutor, public speaking, science and technology days, taster days, judging and demonstrations, home economics day, sports and leisure, certification courses, music and drama, and others. Each of the age groups put Denman College at the top of their wish list, but after that broadly the same pattern of distribution showed trustee training next as preferred choice, with public speaking running as high as home economics and sports. And in each age group there were a fair number who cited certification courses as something they were interested in.

Denman College in Oxfordshire is the WI's residential centre, proclaimed proudly as the only residential centre run by a voluntary organisation. Some 6,000 members attend each year for courses ranging across the entire list quoted above.

When members were asked whether they were using the Institute's range of learning opportunities some 64 per cent said they were. Equally interesting is that 60 per cent of those WI members participated in learning opportunities which were outside of the WI. And then a hugely significant answer was given to a question about where members preferred to hold their meetings. Village halls and community centres topped the list of preferred places.

Although it is well established now, the University of the Third Age (U3A) is the newest voluntary contributor to lifelong learning on the block. The idea began in France in 1972 at a summer school in Toulouse: Université de Troisième Age. It was taken up and introduced here by Peter Laslett, a tireless promoter of adult learning joined by Michael Young (later Lord Young) and Eric Midwinter. Reading off against demography, they realised that there were likely to be increasing numbers of retired people, many of whom would relish both being stimulated through some form of learning as well as those capable of stimulating others, drawing on the experience and knowledge derived from their working lives. The intention was to draw on local expertise and to capitalise on it for the benefit and enjoyment of people living in the area. So it is that there are now some 470 locally based U3As with over 112,000 active members. Each acts as a self-help co-operative of retired men and women who meet to share common interests and a desire to learn for its own sake. Art, foreign languages, music, play reading, creative writing, local history, computing, physical sciences, architecture, bird-watching are all listed as topics pursued in the U3A's background information paper. Some U3As organise visits to theatres, concerts and trips abroad and countryside rambles. Each is likely to have between 150 and 250 members. More often than not they meet monthly in one another's houses, and so the social side of learning is taken care of. Participants come from assorted backgrounds, from people who left school at age 14 with no formal qualifications through to graduates and those with postgraduate qualifications, diplomas and doctorates.

There is another way in which three of these organisations demonstrate how lifelong learning has been evolving. The CAB has already been shown to have close contact with the NOCN. In addition, both the WEA and the WI collaborate with the Oxfordshire Open College Learning Network to have some of their courses validated and accredited so that people who wish to do so can claim OCLN credits. Those credits may go towards achieving some formal qualifications in an increasing number of institutions which accept OCLN credits in some form of credit accumulation system. There was a time when anyone suggesting that following adult education courses could lead to anything approaching a formal public qualification would be laughed out of court. Worse, the very idea that learning for its own sake could be sullied by such vulgar thinking was heresy. Tawney and Mansberg would have a fit; but on reflection perhaps they would not. Since their entire efforts were tuned to the immediate circumstances of their time, were they to be alive now and living in this essentially credentially minded time, it is fair to guess that they would not to stand in the way of people who were seeking to better themselves in ways very different from those which they set out to promulgate. In this way therefore the WEA in itself testifies to the evolving nature and practice of lifelong learning over the past half century.

Accreditation is just the way of the contemporary world. It relates to the public status of the learning activity tied to funding formulae. In addition, accreditation has become and remains a way of ensuring that adult education as offered by voluntary bodies is legitimate, and that learners gain maximum benefit from what they learn. Accreditation for courses offered by voluntary bodies therefore may be seen as a side-effect of the thrust towards the vocational, the instrumental and the funding mechanisms to promote it. Pragmatic as voluntary bodies have to be, if payment by results was now the best way of securing funds then so be it, but only as long as it was kept in its place.

Taking these four voluntary organisations together, a snapshot of their present education activities amounts to a fairly large-scale provision of lifelong learning. The WI has 240,000 members, the WEA 130,000 members, the U3A 120,000 members, the NOCN 663,000 registered learners, the CAB 23,000 volunteers and the National Trust 38,000 volunteers. Not all of those 1,206,000 may be seen as active learners but a very large number are. Even if they are not active, purposeful learners, they are most certainly staying alive as active citizens. They form a vital part of the story of the evolution of the practice of lifelong learning.

Local authorities

This is all the more so when set against the provision of local education authorities for adult education. For 1998 the DfEE Statistical Release for 1999 (SFR 17/1999) shows that about 1.5 million adults enrolled for adult education courses either on a part-time basis or for evening sessions.

Quite apart from its statutory responsibility for providing adult education, LEAs feature in a completely new arena for lifelong learning: governor training. After the 1992 Education Act removed polytechnics from LEAs' responsibility and the incorporation of further education colleges, also removing them from LEA control, schools came next on the devolution map. The grant-maintained schools scheme was invented. Schools were empowered to opt out of LEA control and have a direct financial connection with the DES, renamed the DfEE and now the DfES. This was a particular and further application of local financial management which was applied to all schools. This was necessarily accompanied by a radical overhaul of the way schools were governed. The composition of governing bodies changed, and school governors became legally responsible for the entire range of school activities including its finances. In turn this led to school governors having to deal with a range of issues which formerly had been looked after by the LEA. Similar developments in governor training were undertaken by further education bodies due to the same range of problems being introduced through incorporation.

This list of titles of governor training courses taken from an Inner London LEA autumn programme shows how widely this provision reaches: education funding; governors and inclusion; promoting race equality; interpreting performance data; governors and Ofsted; developing a drugs policy; sex and relationship education: developing a policy; governors' understanding of one's role and responsibilities; Key Stage 3 strategy; chairing meetings: skills for governing; and governors' development.

As from January 2002 there are 17,985 primary schools and 3,457 secondary schools each with its own governing body. At the crudest level of guesswork assuming that most governing bodies will have no fewer than six lay members in primary schools and no fewer than ten lay members in secondary schools, at a conservative estimate this means that across the country there are about 140,000 volunteers acting as governors of schools. This is where the LEAs' provision of governor training comes in. Every time one of those governors attends a governor training session he or she is learning about the law, or the curriculum, or conditions of service for teaching and non-teaching staff or financial management of budgets which often run into many millions of pounds annually. So here again there is a very widespread provision of lifelong learning which rarely features, if at all, in the discourse of the topic.

Non-vocational learning

Add in the provision for learning offered by the National Trust, the Citizens' Advice Bureau, the Women's Institute, the University of the Third Age, not forgetting the continuing if truncated provision by LEAs, and the volume of non-vocational learning becomes impressive. Add in bodies such as the National Extension College, the Open University, the Careers Service, the six residential colleges, the Institute of Personnel and Development, radio and television, prison education, employers themselves and trade unions which are all engaged one way or another in adult learning, and lifelong learning looks in very healthy shape for large sections of the community.

In the background there is a reinvigorated National Institute for Adult Continuing Education (NIACE) acting as a powerful lobbying and developmental agency. It has all LEAs' as members, 134 further education providers, forty-seven higher education providers, professional and national organisations, adult and community education providers, voluntary organisations, arts organisations and awarding bodies. It seeks to promote the study and advancement of adult continuing education, to improve its quality, and to extend participation especially among groups which at present are under-represented. Throughout the period when the vocational threatened to push the liberal out of the way, the NIACE struggled to hold the door open, and has been a central influence in re-establishing the primacy of learning for whatever its purposes, as is now the policy of central government. The NIACE's common sense has helped things progress.

Throughout this evolving story of the shades of different meanings and emphasis, all under the title of lifelong learning, there is an obvious tension between the instrumental provision to contribute to economic requirements as perceived by the government of the day and the open-ended view of learning as propounded by what may still be called liberal education.

Universities and lifelong learning

One of the most telling paradoxes in the story lies in attempts to recruit higher education institutions as providers of vocational preparation. The paradox remains even when attempted interventions by government in the curriculum to promote vocational purposes are glossed with phrases such as employability and work experience. These can certainly be contained within programmes which do not concentrate specifically on getting young graduates ready for employment. But that is not the point. It is this: vocational training purports to have a clearly defined destination. Learning is then about reaching that defined destination. By contrast the essential purpose of a university is to enable students to define their own destinations. Hence it is within universities themselves that any version of lifelong learning becomes a balancing act between the learning related to externally defined destinations and the learning which offers students a route to self-defined destinations.

That tension about lifelong learning rests where it belongs. An essential part of the role of universities is to try to hold that balance, despite all the financial, regulatory and government pressures which tend to oppress them. In the last sentence of the first paragraph in the Chairman's Preface to *Continuing Education From Policies to Practice*, the final report from ACACE (1982), Richard Hoggart (1992) wrote of the way the Committee felt obliged to pay attention to the 'sometimes destructive effects of national and local policy decisions, decisions which were essentially economic rather than educational'.

That was in 1982. Twenty years on and into the twenty-first century, despite their attenuated status, standing and power, universities are the only institutions in the land which can preserve a sense of balance between the economic and educational as a central strand to the evolution of what is meant by lifelong learning. It is only right and proper that it should be so. It is their birthright. They need to be true to it.

They need to be true to it for the population at large. A central purpose of lifelong learning is to enable people to remain in charge of their own lives. Enhancing their skills and employability is a necessary part of the equipment to enable them to do so. But they need more than that. They live on a wider plane than work. They need to be given a chance to determine their own destinations. Fulfilment comes through what feels like a comfortable balance between the publicly instrumental and the privately personal. Learning is one route to that fulfilment. It is not the same route as described by instruction. The institutional tension within universities is thus repeated throughout the land for all its potential lifelong learners. David Blunkett's vision in *The Learning Age* is at the heart of this perception. How far the LSC can help realise it, time alone will tell.

The Learning and Skills Council (LSC)

If Bryan Sanderson, Chairman of the LSC, has anything to do with it, it will not be for lack of effort. In April 2001 he gave a barnstorming lecture at the RSA. He called it 'Unleashing the tiger: will education and training transform the UK?' He talked about branding education. He talked about engaging 'vast armies of new learners'. And the supermarket vigour was on high display:

> Education is not a specialist area; it is a universal issue. And here lies a key proposition: what we are selling – personal transformation – is very much a customer product, but as an industry, we really don't know what our customers think or what they really want. As producers of this particular brand of intellectual capital we can say surprisingly little about the quality of our product in terms which might make the customer want to buy into it.
>
> (Sanderson 2002)

However half-baked much of that is, with its misapplication of managerial jargon to learning which is not and never will be an industry, there is a determination to do something about lifelong learning which runs through it. For that we must be thankful, as we should be for the flat state-ment 'if the LSC is to transform Britain and its people we need to change the way we think'.

Sanderson applies that requirement to the way institutions provide life-long learning at present:

> we need to see them [people] not in our terms – as learners – but as they themselves want to be seen. And maybe we should go further and ask if it is time to reposition our core product – learning.
>
> (ibid.)

So as we move into the twenty-first century, at the official level lifelong learning has been given another twist. Not that the rhetoric does anything to resolve the fundamental tension between the vocational and the non-vocational. Nor does it appear to take significant note of informal learn-ing. But it seems that the energy is there to tackle lifelong learning across a very wide spectrum, and that is a good way to enter the twenty-first century. Perhaps it may herald a more mature approach to adults and their learning.

Nevertheless the tension remains. The LSC will need to be kept up to the mark. And right on cue, Richard Hoggart used his address in October 2001 to the fiftieth anniversary of Glasgow University's Department of Continuing Education to emphasise the central role and responsibility of universities for holding the balance between the vocational and non-vocational for lifelong learning. He noted that adult and continuing edu-cation was now skewed towards the vocational and certificated, and contrasted that with the postwar emphasis which had been on personal development and education for its own sake. He claimed that university departments of continuing education were more needed now than ever before. He continued:

> A lot of people are technically literate, only in the sense that they are open to persuasion and advertising. A democratic society requires critical literacy. The need is as great as ever, if more so, for education for personal, democratic and social life.

That puts the stamp of approval on the notion that now, in some ways, lifelong learning has come full circle. What he does not say he might well have done, is that to ensure that the full circle is closed, the government needs to pay more attention to voluntary bodies than it has done so far. They have been in the business rather longer, they know more about it and they have lessons to offer. A little humility would not go amiss.

So this evolving story ends in 2002 with the theory and practice remaining uncertain. Having gone through all the various permutations of adult, continuing and vocational education, both statutory and voluntary, there is no sense of a settled strategy. There have been increasing numbers of tactical approaches to development by government but nothing to bind them into coherence. And that has to be because lifelong learning is not a policy; it is an aspiration. It is neither fully vocational nor fully general/liberal. It is both and always has been both. A strategy which comprehended that duality with a policy for its implementation is something which as yet we do not have. It is what the next phase of the story needs to be about in the future.

Chapter 4

Catching up

Who are the missing learners?

Who are we talking about? And indeed what are we talking about? These are two sides of the same penny: people on one side and learning on the other. Given the story of the way that lifelong learning has evolved over the last half century both need a sharper focus in trying to work out what lies behind the present emphasis put on it.

Catching up is one way of looking at the issue. Given the very large numbers of people who are engaged in some form of lifelong learning already, it must be other categories of people who are being urged to participate, although there is likely to be some overlap. Given also the economic thrust which informs much of the rhetoric about more people becoming lifelong learners, there is an implicit admission that the country is not where it ought to be. So that rhetoric which from time to time is beamed at the country can be interpreted as an elaborate national game of catch-up in an effort to be where we ought to be. If this is the case then it is important to be clear who we are talking about.

At one end of the scale only one person in four describes themselves as a current learner and only one in three has taken part in education or training since leaving school, with only 14 per cent of employees being involved in job-related training and only one-third of employees claiming that their employers ever offered them any kind of training (Fryer 1997). The English case study in motivating students for lifelong learning in 2000 from the Organisation for Economic Cooperation and Development (OECD) listed one in four adults undertaking current learning, one in three having undertaken no learning since school, with 14 per cent of employees receiving some form of job-related training, one-third of employees never offered anything, 10 per cent of 16-year-olds not in education or employment and 40 per cent of 18-year-olds in no kind of training. The 2000 study by the Basic Skills Agency (BSA) found that 24 per cent of adults in England are functionally illiterate and that the same percentage of the population is innumerate. Simultaneously a comparative study by the OECD found that Britain had more illiteracy than other Anglo-Saxon and European countries. More alarmingly, whereas other countries had illiteracy and innumeracy concentrated among older people, in Britain the literacy problems covered the entire adult age range. For adult literacy Britain was fifth from the bottom of the nine countries in the OECD. And if that was not enough a survey of reading habits plotting the percentages of the population aged 16 to 65 who reported reading a book at least once a month between 1994 and 1998 showed the UK ranked thirteen out of twenty countries. New Zealand, the Czech Republic, Ireland, Germany, Australia, Sweden, Switzerland, Canada, Hungary, the USA, Denmark and Finland ranked one to twelve, respectively. Below thirteenth place were the Netherlands, Poland, Slovenia, Norway, Chile, Portugal and Belgium. Considering the numbers of men and women seen clutching books on public transport and who somehow manage to read them with rapt attention, that list is a sobering commentary on the general literacy level of the population. But at least it begins to lay the foundations.

Or does it? Another OECD study, *Knowledge and Skills for Life, the Programme for International Student Assessment* (PISA) tells a different story. Published in 2001, it gives the results of testing 250,000 15-year-olds across thirty-two countries and records their scores and relative positions on a league table for mathematics, reading and science. It turns out that while not at the top of each league, British youngsters are in the top quarter for reading and maths and just behind Japan, Finland and Korea in science. The mixed news is about the connection between family backgrounds and attainment levels. The study compared the attainments of those coming from the top 25 per cent of occupations with those coming from the bottom 25 per cent. This shows that whereas those in the top 25 per cent were the best in the world at reading, those in the lower occupational groups were just below average. The implication is that the social divide in public education remains one of the most significant factors in accounting for the wide disparity in attainment levels within and across schools.

Regrettable though that is, it is no surprise to anyone who knows anything about primary and secondary schools. Surprisingly that gap is wider in Germany, but for this country the study conveys one alarming piece of information. Some 36 per cent of boys and 29 per cent overall never read for pleasure. The connection with the problems of promoting lifelong learning is obvious. These reading figures are worrying.

The not missing: higher and further education

At the other end of the scale there are the people already engaged in further learning beyond compulsory schooling. So to clear away the foreground to the question who are the missing learners we are talking about, it may be helpful to ask the question the other way round. Who is it that we are not talking about?

At that end of the scale there are now 40 per cent of an age cohort attending higher education. For the academic year 2001 to 2002 there were 365,897 new students admitted to universities, making the total number studying in higher education around two million. Now take the government's targets rising to 50 per cent of those aged under 30 by the year 2005. This means an additional 73,000 students each year. Current discussion as to how to achieve that 50 per cent target begins by noting that some 95 per cent of school leavers with three A levels are already in the system. Thus the additional numbers have to come from somewhere else.

Crudely, there are three possibilities. The first is to increase the number of school leavers who go on to higher education. A 50 per cent target therefore assumes accepting for university places young men and women who do not have the commonly expected three A levels but who may well have less than three or even none. This means that more and more school leavers are to be groomed one way or another for higher education, and that is a lengthy business.

The second is by increasing the numbers of men and women who may have the requisite qualifications but who for one reason or another have not and are not participating, and who are probably in employment. This suggests that they would enrol in higher education essentially on a part-time basis and would need either encouragement or sponsorship to do so from their private sector employers who can see commercial benefit accruing, or by public sector employers who would need to take a much stronger line in supporting the personal as well as professional development of local and central civil servants. This latter is essential. Neither local nor central government has a very impressive record in supporting their personnel in further learning. If private employers are urged to do more, then the government should be setting a rather better example than it is at present.

The third potential source of additional numbers is from relatively recent school leavers who in the jargon are partially qualified but who will need a great deal of persuasion to get them to join in. This is where the wider use of APEL comes into the reckoning. In all probability that means developing the concept of foundation courses further, in effect extending the length of those courses. It also suggests a radical rethink about access courses. When they began, access courses were a deliberate attempt to devise a route for under-qualified men and women from ethnic minorities to qualify as social workers. They did a powerful job in attracting what were inelegantly called 'women returners' and went on to become a highly organised and accredited element in the national coverage. Perhaps now they could serve the same role but with different constituencies. But whichever way it is looked at, the 50 per cent target immediately narrows the field for missing participants in lifelong learning.

This is because with all the emphasis now being put on employability for students in higher education and the government's attempted interference in the curriculum to promote better preparation for work, it seems reasonable to assume that most new graduates will have absorbed the need to continue learning. Even those, who many tutors claim are just going through the motions of learning, being interested solely in getting a qualification with the minimum of effort, will have become aware that in one way or another they are going to have to learn more in the future. If they have not been inoculated with the idea that front-end learning is not going to see them through their working years, they are bound to have picked up via osmosis that in every occupation they can think of, to stay in employment is likely to mean accepting that further learning is one of the conditions for employment.

Still thinking about higher education as those who are not what we are talking about as the missing learners, the latest figures show that for 2002, 54 per cent of the first-year student population in universities and colleges are aged over 21.

There are two other groups concerned with higher education that are not being talked about. Universities have always been vocational to some extent, but since the introduction of the National Council for Vocational Qualifications in 1986 universities have made two distinctive contributions to vocational preparation. First, the Open University's Validation Centre (OUVC) created the Vocational Qualifications Awards Service (VQAS). This was authorised by NCVQ to become a national assessment centre. It issued some 20,000 qualifications a year for bodies such as the National Health Service, the broadcasters' TV skillset, City and Guild staff, and management. It also tried to meet the needs of small professional bodies such as the forensic sciences, transport publishing and criminal intelligence services, but the costs of assessing the vocational qualifications proved prohibitive both for the OU and the professional bodies. Any HEI who wished to offer vocational qualifications through their own courses could turn to the OU's VQAS direct. These men and women are full-blooded participants.

Then the Universities Vocational Awards Council appeared on the scene sponsored and initially funded by Edexcel to provide a service which in effect overlapped with the OU's Vocational Qualifications Awards Service. This body set out to be a university club for handling vocational qualifications but at most it awarded some 20,000 qualifications.

Neither of these bodies has become a major player in the vocational field for the simple reason that NCVQ never managed to produce NVQs at levels 4 and 5, apart from management, which is far and away the largest category for higher education. However, both play a part in higher education's provision for lifelong learning.

The second group are those in mid-career. The rapid and large-scale expansion of postgraduate provision in higher education is a commentary on the way in which the reality of possible career change has affected increasing numbers of people. As many graduates view their career prospects, additional qualifications in management or in their own discipline beckon more insistently. Here is another group of people who are in no sense among the missing, and they are an important category in the universities' contribution to lifelong learning.

Further education colleges have large numbers of students and they too do not come into the missing learner bracket. They will seek to build on the steady improvements shown in hundreds of primary and secondary schools and expand their contribution to further learning. This is not to deny that certain schools do not come up to expectations, but the improvements ought to mean that, in general, literacy and numeracy problems decline among school leavers and so among younger people generally.

All this concerns people who are already engaged in post-secondary school education and who can be claimed loosely to be in the first stages of lifelong learning, with reasonable expectations that a large proportion of them will continue to be long-term lifelong learners.

The not missing: voluntary work and employment

Then there are all those thousands of people referred to in the previous chapter who are engaged in one form of learning or another through voluntary organisations. There are a lot of them. The U3A seems to be the only organisation which tries to find out if its members join in learning activities elsewhere. Its survey of 3,034 members showed that 62 per cent did not. How much overlap there is between the other organisations is impossible to tell. But however much there is, the total number of learning participants in voluntary bodies comprises a considerable proportion of the population aged, say, over 25, bunched as it is bound to be around the 40-plus age group.

In between these two extremes there are hundreds of thousands of employees who need to be continual learners both to retain their own jobs and to ensure that their employing firm or company does not go under. It is impossible to be able to say how far and how many of these employees are or are not lifelong learners. There is a continual battle waged between government and employers on this issue. The government says that employers do not invest enough in education and training courses to remain competitive in the global market. Employers complain about forms, taxation, bureaucracy and about the strength of the pound as a basis for saying that the government does not help them enough.

Yet beneath this argument there is the uncertainty of determining what is and what it not lifelong learning for those in employment. Most employers have some form of induction procedure for new employees. Many will attach a junior to a more experienced worker so that the 'learning by nellie' approach is far from dead, nor could it ever be. Together these may be a very effective way of providing further learning for the employees concerned. How far it actually is will be a reflection of the quality of the management of the firm's department or office. Larger firms will move into a more formal provision for training and the largest will have their own education and training departments. It is those activities which fit the bill for lifelong learning fully because they are easy to count. So it is difficult to say exactly where the 14 per cent referred to in the Fryer Report appear in that range of learning which goes on in employment. It is all the harder because the general agreement that learning now occurs everywhere cannot be taken seriously without accepting that invisible, unquantifiable, on-the-job learning is happening in many workplaces. If it was visible it would count as lifelong learning. Informal learning no less. And it sits half-way along a line drawn from recognisable lifelong learning at one end and the missing at the other.

The not missing: trade unions

Reference has been made already from their very beginnings to the efforts of trade unions to provide opportunities for learning for their members. In addition, there is the latest indication of this commitment in the enthusiastic way some unions have seized the opportunity offered by the introduction of union learning representatives (ULRs). No accurate number of union learners can be quoted, but it is worth repeating that the TUC predicted that by 2012 some 22,000 ULRs would be at work and that through them it was hoped that half a million union members would be involved in some form of LLL. All this would be in addition to the numbers of union members who take advantage of the education opportunities offered by their own union. This means that untold thousands are active participants in lifelong learning.

The missing

So if the above are the groups we are not talking about as missing learners, who are those missing learners? Broadly there are seven groups. There are employees in regular employment; there are women; there are single-parent households; there are the unemployed who are divided further into short-term and long-term jobless; and there are the 16-plus school leavers who tend to move in and out of employment and who often lack a sense of direction. Finally, there are the retired.

Employees in regular employment

The employees missing from anything which constitutes formal lifelong learning are those who are not engaged in some sort of study or training which adds to the capacity of the employer to maintain if not increase the productivity of whatever the activity is, whether manufacturing or service industry, office or shop-floor. All lifelong learning within employment almost by definition has to be vocational and seen by the employer as likely to keep profit figures in the black and avoid getting into the red. Now that the balance between manufacturing and service has changed so dramatically over the past twenty-five years, in practice this means education and training schemes which enhance skills and performance in computing and information technology, repair and maintenance as after-sale provision, personal relationships at work and customer care in all its manifestations whether at the counter in the retail business, hotels or restaurants, on the telephone for help lines, or dealing with customer complaints with an eagle eye on Citizen's Charter provisions; service industries all.

However, that shift in balance between production and service industry does not alter the fact that there are continual anxieties from all areas of employment that there exist serious skill shortages. This points to a key element in the missing, since it is at technician level that this deficiency erupts, and it is difficult to exaggerate the importance of this for the economy. This is a natural arena for further education. How far colleges can manage to fill this gap is one of the current conundrums. Perhaps the Foundation degree will help to fill it. But currently there is no doubt that this is a vital category in the missing.

Over and above all that, somewhere in the urgency attached to the development of lifelong learning in employment is the hope that the capacity for taking the initiative and developing entrepreneurial ideas will be fostered. Sometimes hierarchies prevent bright ideas from working their way upward from those who do the work to those who manage that work. In well-run companies however it is that possibility of a bottom-up flow, of capitalising on bright ideas coming from the day-to-day practice of an employee which can make all the difference to its prosperity.

Employees who are not engaged somewhere in development along these lines are also among the missing lifelong learners. And, given the reports of incompetent or just poor management, there are a substantial number of managers around who can be counted among the missing and who should get themselves out of the missing bracket. They need to perform better. As it is, they contribute to the missing numbers. There are employees at all levels who become avid learners if they are supported, encouraged and treated as adults. Without that they remain among the missing.

Of course it is possible that some employees who claim that their employers have never given them any opportunity for training may attend classes near their homes or follow OU programmes for the sheer pleasure of it, in which case they are not among the missing. But that is not known. They remain among the missing from the ranks of the employees in their workplace.

Women

Despite the increasing numbers of women in higher education and in particular of 'married returners', any employer, if honest, can point to one or more women whom they employ as working way below their capacity. They are far more competent than their existing job requires. Any serious attempt to harness the full potential of the country's working capacity has to pay serious attention to this group of those missing from current arrangements for lifelong learning. They are legion. Time and again, whether it is routing an external enquiry in the right direction, or acting as in-house agony aunt, or offering valuable reminders to a superior, it is these women who make such a significant contribution to performance. Often they tend to remain outside the generally recognised lifelong learning provision because their value goes unrecognised, and they are not encouraged, let alone supported, to develop their capacities further. However, as a group they are highly significant as among the missing from lifelong learning. They are a target for recruitment to its ranks.

But many of the women who are not currently in employment, once were. They take time out for the complicated mixture of motives which are characteristic of all human beings: child-bearing and child-rearing, domestic demands, and personal preference. Not all women want to continue working after they are married irrespective of breeding intentions. Or there are those women who married when they were very young, tired of domesticity and dependent children and want to turn to employment as much as a delayed form of fulfilment as for additional money. Often these women find it hard to enter let alone re-enter the labour market and need some refresher or re-tuning programme to bring their skills and knowledge up to what it is assumed employers need. Here is another group of the missing.

Single-parent households

Then of course there are the considerable number of single-parent households which need to be thought of differently from the unemployed. Indeed they are different from all other groups of missing learners. Many struggle to work out how to combine looking after their homes and with some form of part-time or full-time employment, juggling various categories of benefit in order to do so, and they have to cope with the anxiety and effort required to work out and sustain childcare. It is important to remember too that men as well as women feature as heads of single-parent households. Many, whether men or women, are assumed to have little motivation for work. But whatever their inclinations, this is another group of the missing.

The unemployed

The unemployed are in a different category. Theoretically all unemployed should be in the lifelong learning category. There have been government initiatives galore to train unemployed men and women for jobs. Sometimes it was to train people for specific jobs. More recently, with greatly reduced unemployment, it has been the stick-and-carrot approach, introducing financial penalties in loss of benefit for those who do not turn up for advisory interviews or who reject offers of employment. This is on the grounds that on paper at any rate there are more job vacancies than there are unemployed. But what lies behind this is that employers find that their vacancies exist because they cannot recruit people with the requisite skills. Hence the significance of this group among the missing.

Dividing the unemployed between the long and short term is important in terms of talking about the missing learners. The longer term unemployed tend to be largely men who were laid off from manufacturing and heavy production industries in the middle or second half of their working lives or who become caught up in the ups and downs of the construction industry. Often they became unemployed when unemployment was high and alternative jobs were increasingly difficult to find. As the unemployment figures dropped, if they had not found jobs or had not equipped themselves for whatever jobs were on offer as they grew older, they tended to get left behind as potential employees. As missing learners they are in an unenviable position.

The shorter term unemployed are a shifting group. Generally they are younger, affected by the ups and downs of the economy. Being younger they have more energy to look for alternative employment but often have little inclination to undertake any further training because they think they are going to manage without it, or they do not believe that additional study is going to do anything useful for them. Nevertheless, most are missing and therefore are another target for recruitment into some form of lifelong learning.

The 16-plus school leavers

Then there is one of the most worrying groups of all, namely the continuing cohorts of 16-year-olds, one in ten of whom leave school without any formal qualifications. Amidst all the controversy over A and AS level results in the autumn of 2002, the bleak fact remains that some 30,000 young people left school without any qualifications at all. They are among the 9 per cent who do not get a job and so head for a low-income life in poor housing, likely to pass their disadvantage on to their own children. They tend to be among the trouble-makers in central urban areas and become involved in racial disturbances. Every year which goes by without their being employed makes them a more serious problem both to themselves as well as to society as a whole. Thus as a social issue of exclusion as well as the more straightforward question of employment they form a group which needs to be taken very seriously indeed. The 24 per cent of adults who are illiterate and/or innumerate must therefore come from those two or three groups.

The retired

The retired are obviously in a different category. In some ways they should not feature at all in a discussion about widening participation. In others they are an increasingly significant category of the missing. For them at one level, apart from the fun of it, they have no need of lifelong learning in any formal or vocational sense. At a different level demography suggests otherwise. As an ageing population the problem of balancing tax revenue with expenditure on public services is a tricky task for the Treasury. This is especially so for the National Health Service. Look around any doctor's surgery or waiting rooms in outpatients' departments in hospitals or their geriatric wards. Care and treatment of the ageing and/or aged take up a very large proportion of the available resources.

But demography also suggests that many among the ageing and aged sections of the population will continue working because of shortage of labour. The decline in the value of pensions gives a nasty twist because it suggests that some may have to continuing working. Correspondingly, despite the reluctance of most employers to take on retired men and women as employees, they may have to do so whether they like it or not. Recent discussion about lifting the retirement pensionable age points in that direction. So does the growing tendency of employers to withdraw from their end of employment schemes. Some of the recently retired already have the knowledge and skills as well as the experience to make valued employees, but to make the best use of them many will probably be in the same position as the employed group mentioned above. It is not the case that they can all be dumped in a basket labelled 'You cannot teach an old dog new tricks'. Some can and some cannot learn new tricks. Given the chance many relish the opportunity of doing so, in which case they would cease to be among the missing.

This group of the supposedly retired over-sixties will somehow have to be reduced. By 2025 there will be only two workers for every old person compared with the three for every old person that there are today. The tax system could not sustain the current level of public services with that proportion of people in taxable employment.

Catching up or caught up?

Perhaps the most interesting way of considering all the above groups who for these purposes may be thought of as missing from the ranks of the lifelong learning is to wonder whether it might be a declining issue. Seeing the joiners against the non-joiners begins with the 50 per cent target for higher education. Add in the large numbers who are already engaged in some form or other of lifelong learning either through further education colleges or voluntary bodies. Add in too the numbers of employees who are invisible learners through their on-the-job learning.

Then take the relatively successful efforts of the government from 1997 to lift the standards and levels of achievement in primary schools in literacy and numeracy. Notice that those efforts are now being applied to secondary schools with the avowed intention of ensuring that pupils leave school properly equipped for employment. Since young people are so heavily influenced in their attitudes towards engagement in lifelong learning by their experience of learning in school, could it be that their ever-increasing numbers will move quite naturally into lifelong learning of whatever kind is suitable for them as they grow and mature? That may be a false hope. Certainly it will not be realised without serious reconsideration of what schools are for.

In other words, is the current rhetoric about lifelong learning really a complicated exercise of playing catch-up? Demography, rising standards in schools and expanding post-secondary education participation ought to mean that it could become less of a problem. It is needed urgently to make up for previous deficiencies and it is a highly complex enterprise to turn rhetoric into successful activity. But if lifelong learning is going to be successful there must be something in it which triggers the interests of the missing learners. In other words, there has to be something to motivate them. That something has to be more expansive, more imaginative than thinking narrowly about vocational education and training.

What counts as lifelong learning?

This raises the curriculum issue of what counts as lifelong learning and what does not. If there is learning going on which does not accord with the accepted views of what is included as lifelong learning, those learners cannot be thought of as missing.

If the missing learners are anywhere nearly contained in the groups referred to, what learning is it assumed they need to undertake? What learning is being talked about? This can be sorted out in a variety of ways.

Whichever way it is resolved, it is vital to distinguish learning from education and training. Education and training are processes which may or may not lead to learning. And whichever way the sorting goes, learning comprises a complex mixture of knowledge, skills and abilities, all of which is pretty obvious, but it also refers to attitudes and behaviours which are not so readily thought of as learning.

One way of dividing up learning into different categories is to refer to formal learning, non-formal learning and informal learning. The Institute of Employment Studies' *Adult Learning in England: A Review* (Hillage *et al.* 2000) offers this neat distinction drawn from adult education literature. Formal learning for that publication is 'learning which is undertaken within formal education institutions'. Non-formal learning is 'organised, systematic learning carried on outside the framework of the formal system'. Informal learning is 'learning which occurs frequently in the process of daily living, sometimes coincidentally, although it can be accredited through systems of recognition of prior experiential learning (APEL), and some of its outcomes can be evaluated'. The Review goes on to quote McGivney's operational definition of informal learning as 'learning that takes place outside a dedicated learning environment, which arises from the activities and interest of individuals or groups but which may not be recognised as learning'. (McGivney 1999).

Immediately this points to some of the confusion which arises when talking about lifelong learning. Does paying attention to the legal, financial as well as the organisational requirements of an application to the lottery for funds count as learning if it is all based on experience and is in no way the result of being told how to do it? Does the success in mastering the administrative skills required for running a large fishing or sailing club which results from experience and from learning how to do it from someone who has retired, count?

Classifying formal learning is straightforward. *The National Adult Learning Survey* (NALS) (Beinart and Smith 1997) listed ten categories of learning to cover what it called taught learning and non-taught learning. For taught learning it listed:

- Any taught courses that were meant to lead to qualifications.
- Any taught courses designed to help develop skills that might be used in a job.
- Any courses, instruction or tuition in driving, playing a musical instrument, in an art or craft, in a sport or any practical skill.
- Evening classes.
- Learning which has involved working on one's own from a package of materials provided by an employer, college, commercial organisation or other training provider.
- Any other taught course, instruction or tuition.

The last category seems a catch-all to include anything which anyone else might think of, though it is hard to know what!

The NALS then listed the following to cover non-taught learning:

- Studying for qualifications without taking part in a course.
- Supervised training while doing a job (i.e. when a manager or experienced colleague spends time helping an individual to learn or develop skills as they do specific tasks at work).
- Time spent keeping up to date with developments in the type of work done without taking part in a course (e.g. reading books, manuals or journals or attending seminars).
- Deliberately trying to improve one's knowledge about anything or teaching oneself a skill without taking part in a taught course.

These lists were the result of efforts to produce questions in a survey which was intelligible to recipients concerning their activities as self-directed learners without including 'such a wide range of human experience as to render our definition nearly meaningless'.

Taught learning as formal learning is clear. Non-taught learning is clearly different and its overlap with informal learning is also clear, but the non-taught learning list certainly does not cover the definition offered by McGivney. None of this is much help in working out what lifelong learning really means in its present usage because much of it is not countable. This leads to another way of dividing up learning into vocational and non-vocational learning. The first is taken to mean any kind of learning which relates to a job or occupation. The second refers to everything else. But that is seeking to say what it purports to be for rather than what it is. It is a rerun of the debate about what is relevant or useful learning as opposed to all other learning. That debate shows up in the Preface to *The Learning Age* (DfEE 1998a) referred to in the previous chapter. The humanitarian, liberal view of lifelong learning is firmly stated there, but so are the economic concerns which emphasise the need for more vocational learning. It is inevitable that governments will call for more vocational learning whether or not they recognise the need for a wider view of lifelong learning as a life-enhancing business. But it begs the central question.

What is the vocational learning which relates directly to a job or occupation? It used to be the case that the Civil Service recruited heavily from graduates who had read classics at universities. An outstandingly successful medical school in MacMaster University in Canada recruits deliberately from applicants who have not read science in their undergraduate studies. Contemporary employers will often say that they are not particularly interested in what a newly graduated applicant studied. They are far more interested in an ability to grasp issues quickly, to show flexibility in their general approach to things, to communicate effectively both aurally and on paper, to work in teams and now of course by using IT. So if the applicant read theology or geography or philosophy, where is the vocational strand to their university studies? The government has attempted to bridge this alleged gap by trying to persuade universities to include deliberate preparation for employment in their curricula. Thus at higher education level the vocational can be covered generally by the concept of employability, but that only evades the distinction between useful and other learning.

The same approach may be applied to almost any trade, work or occupation. A plumber is taught about pipes, joints, pressures, levels, central heating, all kinds of equipment, building regulations and the way local authorities apply them, materials and, with luck, something about cash flow. Take two plumbers who went through the same course at the same time and who currently both work in private houses. One lists the customer's requirements and sets about installing the equipment in an efficient, quick, cost-effective way, following the customer's instructions to the letter. The other lists the customer's requirements but, in setting about the job, realises that there is something which may or may not be intentional but which needs checking. It may be the way a central heating pipe is run around a room; it may be the positioning of a wash-basin in relation to the borrowed light from a window. The plumber knows that unless he checks this out there is a risk that the customer will be dissatisfied with the results of his work. Whatever it is, it needs to be checked with the customer. This is not something which can be taught as such, but it is a vital ingredient in the plumber's vocational performance. He may have picked it up from his wife after making some blunder at home or it may be because he paints in watercolours as a hobby and so has acquired a sensitive attitude to the appearance of things. Whatever it is, that customer is lucky. It is the same as the classicist or the non-science applicant for medicine at MacMaster University. A vital part of vocational performance has nothing to do with specific vocational preparation. It has everything to do with an ability to think and an interest in doing so.

Another way of straddling the vocational and the non-vocational divide is to say that it does not matter a jot what is learned or how it is learned so long as something is being learned because, more often than not, it shows that the mind is working actively. But that runs into the difficulty of counting results for funding purposes under the current arrangements because such learning is impossible to quantify. Quality is still more difficult to deal with.

Whether the Learning and Skills Council (LSC) will lead to improvements in understanding what is the wisest balance between useful and other learning and how to enrol the missing in either, time will tell. People are on one side of the coin and what is learned is on the other.

The LSC's regional structure ought to help but that is an open question. If it is going to engage more employers as active promoters of lifelong learning and, through them, persuade individual employees of its value, then it is going to need to find approaches which are different from those which have been tried before. They need to be consonant with the nature of being adult. Motivation is the key.

The Chairman Bryan Sanderson seems to understand this. His opening sentences in his RSA lecture are as follows:

> Learners is a word we use all the time. Everyone who reads articles like this is, in a sense, a learner. It is a curious fact though that seeing people as learners seems to be something of an obstacle for the Learning and Skills Council. The reason it's a problem is that the people we're trying to reach don't see themselves that way. They don't think of themselves as Learners. So why do we continue to use the term – and follow an approach founded in learning culture – when it's patently obvious we're not connecting with the vast majority of the population.... Learning is about directional self development. It's about realising potential, positive change, the acquisition of knowledge and ideas.
>
> (Sanderson 2002)

That sounds like an employer who is more interested in applicants who show some aptitude for acquiring new capabilities than those with a neat vocational training. He will find uncertain acceptance in some of the reaches of the LSC. But perhaps the debate about what constitutes lifelong learning has moved on several steps.

However, there is another category of the missing which is another way of looking at learning: employers. How can it be that, despite decades of being urged to be more active in providing training for their employees, far too many appear not to have learned of its necessity, or if they have learned then they have passed it up as inessential for them?

Thus on the one hand there are the people who are missing from lifelong learning whether or not they are called learners; on the other hand there is whatever constitutes self-development, potential change and new learning. When this is stripped of its rhetoric it amounts to saying that one problem of lifelong learning and its missing participants lies in the wider issue of social exclusion. In some ways the anxiety about lifelong learning is an extended essay on the danger, misery and hopelessness of social exclusion.

But there is another problem about the missing in the context of social exclusion: the shifting boundaries between different groups of people. The obvious widening of the gap between people who are in work and live quite comfortably and the poor could mean that a sizeable number of men among the poor are neither in work nor even seek it. That group could get smaller if some were engaged in learning which would help them find employment. But it could grow larger if the trends in employment lead to requirements for employees to have higher qualifications to reflect the increased sophistication of working practices which in their turn could reduce the number employed. Men could be more vulnerable to any such developments than women. In other words, in a society characterised by fluidity between different groups, social exclusion can be a more complex issue than applying the concept to the existing poor. Hence there is no way of knowing who next year's missing might be.

This is the most disturbing way of thinking about the missing. Behind all the speculation about who is in and who is out of lifelong learning, the one certainty is that it is among the poor where the largest groups of the missing are to be found. Not to try to do something to tackle that very difficult area of lifelong learning would be an ethical disgrace. Trying to do something means treating as adults individuals who may be poor but who, like others, have their own needs which need to be met and respected. They are vulnerable in ways which separate them from the rest of society but they are also part of it. If lifelong learning is going to connect with this group of the missing it has to be through finding ways of identifying possible motivations as beginning points and seeking to build on them.

Clearly, lifelong learning will never be thoroughly caught up; the world of work and living is changing too fast for that. But if the problems of social exclusion encompass large numbers of the missing, it is also clear that the notion of catch up means lifelong learning as 'realising potential, positive change, the acquisition of knowledge and ideas' which runs way beyond any interpretation of the vocational. To realise this in practice has to mean treating adults as adults whatever their position in society, in grown-up institutions, with financial regulations which are intended to support and help correct the mismatch between what is on offer and rejected and the participation desired. The numbers of the missing might just then be smaller. Joined-up government would help.

Chapter 5

Motivational mismatches for lifelong learning

Why do the missing learners continue to be missing? In shorthand terms the answer is that there is a mismatch all round. It is not just the obvious mismatch between adults and how they would benefit if they learned on the one hand, and cold, dreary buildings, uncongenial fellow learners, and, even worse, uncongenial teachers on the other. Nor is it just a curriculum which does not mesh with people's preoccupations. More than that there are far-reaching mismatch features which reach down into society. And they are not only the obvious sociological factors. There are far deeper psychological, pedagogical as well as institutional mismatches which run right through any way of looking at lifelong learning for the majority. And they create a serious range of obstacles to the admirably high aspirations of recent government policies.

The missing

It is vital to remember who are the missing learners we are talking about and who are caught up in the mismatches. They are not those who are involved in any of the vast range of experiences which may or may not be concerned explicitly with learning but which come under any interpretation of lifelong learning. One way or another, those people have managed to use, circumvent or override any psychological, pedagogical or institutional obstacles they might encounter. The vital point is that they did not have to do so. They *chose* to do so. They had the knowledge and skills and the confidence to enable them to do so, to know how to set about finding opportunities for whatever it was they wanted to learn about.

Many of the missing have little or none of that equipment. In any case, the majority of them are probably unaware of the mounting crescendo of expectations that are beamed at them, urging their participation, nor do they grasp its importance for them as individuals. And, being information poor, they are stuck in a different groove in the mismatch.

The point is made succinctly in *Creating Learning Cultures* (NAGCELL 1999). Paragraph 3.6 reads:

in our country today, far too many people are still locked in a culture which regards lifelong learning as either unnecessary, unappealing, uninteresting or unavailable. Once schooling or immediate post school education is over, they want nothing more of learning than it should largely leave them alone.

Now why is that? It applies to 'far too many', yet not to all. Clearly, where it does apply, it goes back to schooling. Thus there are psychological, pedagogical and institutional factors which most certainly influence if not actually control subsequent attitudes to any form of learning after leaving school. In order to understand the reluctance of the missing to become visible in lifelong learning terms it is necessary to go back to the beginning.

Schools

When the provision of schools for all began in the nineteenth century, to all intents and purposes the curriculum was a watered-down extension of what went on in the classrooms of the independent public schools. Beyond the basic skills without frills, or the three Rs as they used to be called, there was little in the classroom experience of the boys and girls who went to Board and later named Council schools which connected with the working lives they were to live after school, other than to give them clerking or shop assistant skills or consigning them to the ranks of the unskilled. While the world of factory production developed apace, with its increasingly sophisticated engineering and technological skills outside the walls of the school, inside those walls the world of learning for young people continued as if those developments were not happening. As long as clerks could add and write legibly then the job was done. The unskilled did not need much education as labourers anyway. A little history and geography could be thrown in by rote. So just as the idea of engineering, technology and anything specifically vocational was anathema to public schools, so that view of the curriculum was thrust on to everyone else. With few exceptions, the education system was preparing its pupils for a working world which was fast leaving it behind.

This was all done with the best of intentions. The trouble was that the people who had responsibility for creating, organising and administering the schools' system had nothing but their own public school experience to go on. That experience served them very well. However, the disdain for manufacturing and industry with which they were inoculated during their school years was applied to schools for everyone else. It served them very badly. The trouble was and still is that it set up the contentious argument about the relationship, role and place of the academic and the vocational which rumbles on to this day. And the fact that it rumbles on bedevils current debates about lifelong learning, nearly a hundred and fifty years later.

A narrow curriculum meant a narrow pedagogy and a narrow place to conduct it: desks in rows, boys and girls segregated by rows if not in separate rooms; canes to keep learning moving by rote; strict discipline the order of the day; all in buildings which more often than not looked not unlike the factories those boys and girls would subsequently be working in.

Psychologically, pedagogically and institutionally, in some ways some of those influences continue today. The world outside has changed faster and gone further than the way schools are organised, constrained as they are nowadays by a never-ending stream of regulations as they try to provide the best possible service for their pupils.

Catch-up for schools, students and parents

Just as there can be a 'catch-up' way of looking at the missing from life-long learning, so also there can be a 'catch-up' way of looking at schools. The need is obvious. It ought to have been blindingly obvious for a quarter of a century. Had it been acted upon earlier, the position of the missing would not be what it is today.

Since the end of the Second World War there has been little success in realising the vision which was articulated in the Butler Act, for creating a secondary education system which was consonant with the requirements of a modern industrial society, beyond numbers of secondary schools and numbers of pupils in them, great achievements though they were. In retrospect it still seems astonishing that secondary schooling for all has existed for only about half a century. It is difficult to keep that in perspective. Up until the 1880s schooling lasted up to age 8. But it is even more astonishing that politicians failed to understand that the successful rebuilding of the nation's postwar economy depended on expanding rapidly its industrial and production base which in turn could only be done by providing a flow of young people who had some technological preparation for the working world they were destined to enter. Instead, whatever the good intentions, once again there was an over-emphasis on the academic provision of grammar schools. Prestige of academic study and parental aspirations went with them. The small number of technical schools which were created under the tripartite schools of the Act were insufficient to redress the balance between academic and vocational education. Thus about 90 per cent of the school-aged population went to secondary modern schools which at best more often than not provided a continuation of the general education idea aped in part from the grammar schools and at worst were extensions of the former elementary schools when the leaving age was 14. They were engaged in preparing young people for the working world as it was but which was changing fast. With few exceptions they did not engage with preparations for the working world to come. That would have required a systematic development of schools with a vocational bias in which the same emphasis would have been given to technical, science and engineering which was given to academic study in grammar schools. Again in retrospect, perhaps it would have been better for Butler to have thought about two kinds of secondary schools and not three.

As it is, the failure to square this circle has bedevilled education development ever since. David Eccles' White Paper in 1956, *Technical Education*, tried to engage with the issue. Anthony Crosland's 10/65 Circular was another attempt to correct the balance by going as far as he dared in replacing grammar schools by demanding from local education authorities plans for the reorganisation of secondary schools along comprehensive lines. Whatever its purposes it led to contentious arguments with local education authorities which did little to advance the cause of technical education.

But worse, right through there has been a concentration on institutional structures and reorganisation of systems. Until very recently there has been little attempt in policy terms to think out what the newly created institutions were for. Little attention was paid to what was supposed to be going on inside them; in other words, the curriculum. Following Jim Callaghan's 'secret garden' speech at Ruskin College in 1976, the first time that a Prime Minister had said anything important about education in public, Baker's 1988 Education Act tackled the curricula issue with the introduction of a National Curriculum and invented technology colleges to boot. Clarke's Education Act of 1992 added a highly interventionist version of inspection to oversee the workings on the National Curriculum and attend to the standards of achievement being reached. General National Vocational Qualifications fared not much better as a means of attracting secondary school pupils to a vocational version of higher education. More recently, the introduction of possibilities for schools to specialise in technology as well as in the arts and humanities has taken those developments to another level. But however effective those measures may be in benefiting the majority of secondary school pupils, this is where many begin their lives as the missing from lifelong learning.

To corral in classrooms young men and women who have no interest in being there is asking for trouble when they are interchangeable in height, weight, shape and sheer size with those a year older who are walking around in the real world. Institutionally both the facilities and the framework of the day leave little time and no space for personal choices to be made, to help develop a sense of who they are and what they want. It is small wonder that many develop subtle forms of rebellion which become inimical thrusts against learning. All this makes it more difficult to find ways of keeping them interested in learning.

Pedagogical issues follow. Requiring young men and women to settle down in their mid-adolescence to study for examinations which are not framed with their interests in mind, to learn about subjects which are of little or no interest to them, and with homework thrown in, is hardly the best way to send them out into the world as enthusiastic learners. Indeed it is hardly the best way to ensure that they attend school regularly. A great deal of fuss is made about truancy and attendance these days. Attendance percentages are used as a measure for assessing a school's overall performance. But when all the electronic devices have been installed, and highly sophisticated arrangements established for registration and contacting parents, the central question remains: Why are they not there? All too often they are not there because of the nature of the curriculum which is served up to them every day they are in school. They do not want to be there.

All this goes back to an over-emphasis on systems, structures and organisation. As far as pupils are concerned these are abstractions which have little to do with them. And the tragedy is that those preoccupations tend to divert attention from finding ways of answering the vital question: What would it be in the pupils' best interests for them to learn? If life in the classroom was interesting and engaged them, instances of truanting would fall.

Unhappily this is where the missing begin to go missing. Peer group pressure, petty crime, drugs, smoking where it is forbidden and simply hanging about in the streets can so easily lead to truanting which becomes a high-octane game, a way of life which is a guaranteed way of ensuring that they are likely to join the ranks of the missing lifelong learners. Boredom has to be filled with something.

Even worse, all this is so damaging psychologically. Again take the classroom. Adults thrive on encouragement, support, appreciation and a sense of a job well done. So do adolescents. And, like adults, they do not flourish if they are continually confronted by their own failures and inadequacies. All the confusions of leaving childhood behind and becoming something else are bad enough. If a sense of failure is how they experience their time at school, that sense of identity is confused even further with the risk of the classic response setting in as self-defence. If you do not try you cannot be a failure. Once that defensive tactic sets in, it is often a miracle if anything positive results from efforts by imaginative teachers to bring the young man or woman in from the cold. Again this is where many of the missing begin to go missing. In no way is this a criticism of what schools and their teachers are attempting to do. They have no choice in the curriculum which they are required to follow with their students. It is more to do with a system which cramps their style. Nowadays there is little or no scope for the unconventional teachers who can somehow find a way of encouraging learning by the obvious if difficult means of accepting who and what their pupils are as the starting point for learning more. A few years on, and these are the people at whom bland-ishments about lifelong learning are aimed. It is small wonder that they are not enthusiastic joiners.

Meanwhile, their parents and large parts of their parents' parents' generation have not dissimilar recollections of their schools. They may not have been truants or in any way troublesome pupils, but, for all too many, they left school convinced that they were pretty hopeless as learners. Later in life the memories of their school experience tend to put them off having anything to do with formal education: Why run the risk of being a failure again? The sad truth is that the mismatch set up in school is carried over into later life as a set of perceptions about themselves as well as educational institutions. In addition, it is just as well to recall at every stage of discussion about lifelong learning that home and peer group influence is as, if not more, important than school in determining atti-tudes to learning.

The mismatched world of the missing

No wonder the NAGCELL Report says that too many people 'are still locked in a culture which regards lifelong learning as either unnecessary, unappealing, uninteresting or unavailable'.

Trying to come to terms with the complications of lifelong learning and to relate them to the world in which people actually live, the second report of the NAGCELL, *Creating Learning Cultures* (1999), had a whole section entitled 'The risk society'. In a way it indicates the kind of world in which those influences are still running their course. But it also sets out some of the day-to-day factors which many of the missing lifelong learners find themselves having to cope with.

The risk society: factors contributing to it

- Accelerating change in many dimensions of life from work to the family driven in part by powerful and often remote global forces.
- Increasing diversity and fragmentation of experiences and institutions and a greater willingness to tolerate even celebrate such features of the modern world.
- Changing identities, loyalties and aspirations.
- Much greater emphasis upon consumption and its pleasures, includ-ing too some democratisation of inventiveness and creativity.
- More focus upon choice, lifestyle and individuality.
- The increasing variety and pluralism of popular culture.
- The pervasive and growing role of information and knowledge in many arenas of economic, social, political and working life.

- The growing importance of communications and information techno-logy to many aspects of our lives.
- The development of new dimensions of political participation, in the realms of constitutional reform and active citizenship.
- The emergence of new agendas in politics, concerned with issues as diverse as race and gender equality, disability rights, the environment, food and transport.
- A widening of key social divisions, experienced in fields of income, employment, housing, health and education, including access to information.
- Evidence of the growth of social exclusion, despair and even a sense of hopelessness, resulting from the impact of multiple deprivations.

(NAGCELL 1999)

This amounts to saying that almost every single aspect of living in the twenty-first century has changed for good. Whereas there were certainties in the past, now there are practically none. Where there used to be under-stood hierarchies as boundaries within which people lived, there is now a social fluidity which hugely benefits a large part of the population, but which can leave the missing feeling ignored and on the sidelines of every-thing. The fragmentation of institutions has seen to that. Family, work-place, church, all function differently from when they were established features on the living landscape, offering a range of connections with other people, effortlessly, naturally, incidentally, easily.

With a job for life gone, and the decline of production and heavy smoke-stack industry which used to provide jobs for unskilled labourers and the social life that went with it, many men are left without many of the kinds of personal security and social structure which previously they took for granted. Without that, or at least a job which made them feel like proper men, many feel emasculated, their principal role in life taken from them, their position in the family diminished. It is like a rite of passage reversed.

Add to that list the remarkable development in the role women have played in society over the past twenty-five years and the topsy-turvy nature of life begins to come into focus. Wherever, whatever the context, women are increasingly doing jobs which only a relatively short time ago were done exclusively by men. Bus, train and taxi driving, construction work on building sites, railway station managing, combatant roles in the armed forces, engineering; in every imaginable profession women are fast per-forming a vital function in keeping the economy and society running without which life would grind to a halt. In addition to the uncertainties of employment affecting both men and women are the anxieties about redundancies resulting from worldwide activities of great corporate com-panies and the ups and downs of the contemporary versions of the global economy. Add in too the debilitating experience of unemployment, and beneath it all there is the mysterious and little understood shift in the patterns of relationships between men and women, affecting society as a whole.

Set all this amid the continual rise, experienced almost universally, in living standards and their effect on domestic budgets; then try to construct a mental picture of what goes on in many families. The man is worried about his job, and may or may not fulfil his role properly as parent, child escort to school or domestic helper. The woman comes in from work, also worried about her job, exhausted, and sets about being mother, caterer, perhaps shopper and house organiser. Meanwhile the children have their expectations heightened by what they see on television and make a fuss if these expectations are not met – instant gratification is rampant – and there may be problems with childminding arrangements and worries about children's safety going to and from school. This is the world in which increasing numbers of people live. Yet, due to the influence of inflation over the past twenty-five years, there is an assumption born of experience that somehow next year ought to be better than this year. Now that inflation is so low even that assumption lies in tatters. The price of all this is strain and stress writ large for many people.

All this tends to bear down more harshly on the missing lifelong learners. Not being on the inside track of events, like at least 50 per cent of the population, many are ill-equipped to deal with some of the risks they have to navigate. Think of the single parent in relation to that almost frightening list of risk factors above, and the point is made. On the one hand there is an urgent need for individuals to have the knowledge and confidence required to help in coping which lifelong learning has to offer. On the other, many tend to be numbered among those who are still locked 'in a culture which regards lifelong learning as either unnecessary, unappealing, uninteresting or unavailable. Once schooling or immediate post school education is over, they want nothing more of learning than it should largely leave them alone'.

Nor is this all there is to mismatching. One of the most far-reaching developments which impinges on lifelong learning is the rapid and extensive alteration in the division between the accepted responsibilities of the state and those of the individual. Whatever the balance of argument between those who welcome the decline of what they label a dependency society and those who fear the effect of progressive withdrawal of the state from the provision of essential services, there is no doubt that the crudities of the 'on your bike' mentality in all its manifestations tend to bear down hardest on the very people who could be so well served by lifelong learning. Health, education, pensions, the labyrinth of benefits, all add to the burden of those who are not on the inside track.

This is the world in which the reluctant school pupils who are potentially among the missing adult learners are going to live. What is to be done about this is explored later. Here it is worth recording that the length of compulsory schooling, the influence of the regulations about how the National Curriculum is fulfilled, the effect of league tables, the paperwork imposed by central government, all result in teachers being unable to use their own judgement as professionals as to what they consider might be best for any group of pupils. The 'one size fits all' makes it almost inevitable that some pupils will become among the legions of the missing from lifelong learning. Albeit unintentionally, the government may have increased the numbers of the missing.

'Unnecessary, unappealing, uninteresting or unavailable'

It is not only secondary school pupils and school leavers who are affected by this rapidly changing world. Their parents, uncles and aunts, cousins and peer groups are potential learners as well. These are the people for whom lifelong learning is 'unnecessary, unappealing, uninteresting or unavailable'. This is a fairly devastating indictment of lifelong learning as it is perceived by a large section of the population. It means that thousands of men and women reckon that lifelong learning has nothing to do with them. It means that they see no particular reason to take the idea of learning more seriously. Getting a job through becoming more employable, getting better at dealing with the domestic budget and so avoiding angry accusations of blame, improving children's health through knowing more about the nutritional values of different foods or their education, making better sense of the rules and regulations which govern benefit entitlements; even if an attractive brochure came through the letterbox offering learning opportunities about topics such as these, ones which would engage with some of the issues that concern them directly, it is highly unlikely that they would pay sufficient attention to begin thinking about enrolling, not to mention adopting the frame of mind which would take them to a college to do so.

As with adolescents who are disenchanted with the learning provided by school, fundamentally this is talking about the curriculum for potential lifelong learners. 'Unnecessary' means that nothing provided under the heading of lifelong learning has anything to offer them which is worthwhile.

'Unappealing and uninteresting' are cousins to 'unnecessary'. For something to be appealing almost by definition it is bound to be interesting. If learning opportunities are seen to be unappealing and uninteresting it is no wonder that they are considered 'unnecessary'. It is difficult to avoid the conclusion that part of the problem with lifelong learning lies in what is considered a proper learning diet for the missing.'

Then there is 'unavailable'. This word can be used to describe a long list of obstacles to the missing becoming visible learners. Time, place and space are almost defining factors making for unavailability. Take place first. Even though there have been important moves away from the automatic assumption that learning opportunities are provided in institutions and that people who wish to learn must come to them, generally speaking the bulk of what is provided as lifelong learning through further education colleges is based on that assumption. So even if some of the missing get around to thinking about joining a lifelong learning class or activity, all too often it means plucking up enough courage to travel some distance and confront horrors from earlier schooling. For many it is like going into foreign territory, and there have to be some very good reasons for doing that. More often than not the building itself is not very inviting, either from the outside or the inside. Well-tended grounds and premises imply respect and care for those who come to it. That is no more than good manners. And they do not have to be brand new buildings to do that. Scruffy premises seem fit for scruffy people. Inside, the sight of long, unyielding corridors with classrooms off them containing rows of desks and chairs, can be not merely off-putting but positively discouraging. Just as the wrong furniture can tip disenchanted adolescents in school over the boundaries of reasonable behaviour because they detest thinking they are being treated like children, so for adults the wrong furniture sends the wrong messages. It is too near the adage that learning has to be hard work if it is to be real learning, and not close enough to the idea that learning can be enjoyable as well as requiring effort.

It is another instance of how education is so out of step with much of our living environment. Apart from the very poor, most homes offer reasonable comfort, and what is not actually present is experienced vicariously through pictures on the television screen. Yet educational institutions remain essentially uncomfortable places to be in, and it need not be so. Hence not only is place important when thinking about lifelong learning but so is space. For adults, thinking about place and space is essential. They need both and there needs to be welcoming place and space.

But even if the buildings and rooms are inviting, more often than not they are not next door. Getting there can be a serious problem. And it is not just fitting the time for a class around domestic and work responsibilities, for those having to use public transport travel may be a major obstacle. And it costs money. If a potential lifelong learning participant is diffident about approaching a college to begin with, those travel problems can be enough to deter people for life.

This leads on to time. Whether it is morning, noon, night or evening, for many of the missing discussed so far it is almost impossible to find the time to get out of the house to attend a course or activity because of the pressures on families at home. This is particularly true for single mothers. Unless there is a willing neighbour or inexpensive baby-sitter, however strong the will to engage with further learning it may be literally impossible.

On top of all that there are regulations. One of more bizarre factors affecting lifelong learning is that one set of government regulations prevents the implementation of public policy from a different department. There is talk about joined-up government. Lifelong learning is an example of where there appears to be none. Rather, think disjointed government. It is like a devil's cocktail. Encourage people to make full use of benefit entitlement. Encourage the same people to earn. Add a strong dose of urging people to engage in lifelong learning. Spice with benefit rules which punish people for earning more than a pittance and forbid them to learn for more than specified hours a week. Serve up as a poisonous brew and hope that those who can be persuaded to drink it have a built-in filtration system which spews out the offending ingredients, leaving them alive and ready to learn.

For decades this has been one of the most balmy aspects to the entire thrust by government to promote more education and training. And for the missing in the current discussion it is almost as if some malignant force is at work within government to make further learning as difficult as possible for the very people it urges to participate, and who need it most because they are the most vulnerable.

Mismatched employers and employees

So far, the question why are the missing missing has been addressed to those who can loosely be called the disenchanted. But if only 14 per cent of employees are sponsored by their employers in one way or another to undertake some form of further learning, why are the other 80 per cent of employees missing?

For a start, as remarked above, large numbers of them are not missing at all. They are busy learning through every form of voluntary activity imaginable, where learning is mixed up with volunteering. It may be in the Citizens Advice Bureau, the Women's Institute, the National Trust, Neighbourhood Watch, community activity, village halls, or it may be through pursuing further learning explicitly through the WEA or local authority classes. None of this may be the kind of vocational lifelong learning which features so prominently in government rhetoric, but it is lifelong learning notwithstanding. For these people, whatever they do is clearly neither unappealing nor uninteresting but the opposite, and therefore there is no sense in which they feel that learning is unnecessary. They are not in the category of wanting 'nothing more of learning than it should largely leave them alone'. Their minds are at work. They are making an effort to engage in some activity which is additional to the rest of their lives.

Even subtracting that unquantifiable number from the 86 per cent of employees who do not follow any further education or training, it leaves a very large number who fall into the category of missing. For many of them too, any form of lifelong learning is 'unnecessary, unappealing, uninteresting or unavailable'. Why should that be so?

Probably the most important reason is that too many employers do little or nothing to encourage them. This is a mystery which so far no one has penetrated. It has to point to some mismatch between need for further learning and complacency, or contentment with the current performance of the organisation on the part of employers, or even laziness about retraining needs. If there is no financial support forthcoming for employees then it is down to individuals. This is particularly true for small and medium-sized businesses. With a very small profit margin for many and a relatively small number of employees, employee development as a budget item can threaten the viability of a firm. But the number of people who need a push to get on with something far outweighs the number of self-starters who will do things for themselves because they want to for any one of a complex range or reasons. So if there is no financial support it is the level of individuals' motivation which governs those who do and those who do not participate in lifelong learning.

The eighty-two Training and Enterprise Councils which were established in the late 1980s aimed to promote employee development and support the economic development of their area. They were meant to nudge more employers into providing training for their employees. Some commentators speculated that if they failed, perhaps legislation would make it compulsory for employers to engage their employees in further training. Nothing of the kind has happened. Their relative failure led in part to the creation of the Learning and Skills Council but it leaves open the question of how to persuade more employers to take training seriously and budget for it. Now nearly twenty years later Leslie Wagner, Vice-Chancellor of Leeds Metropolitan University who chairs the Universities Vocational Award Council, wondered aloud if some coercion was now necessary. This has to be the measure of the continuing need for employee development schemes, especially in engineering and information technology. There remains a bewildering mismatch between the training requirements which are acknowledged and the participation levels which remain relatively low.

Those who are strongly motivated can see further learning as a springboard for advancement, as intrinsically interesting and stimulating, as a deliberate engagement with something to do with personal growth and development, health and fitness or as an enjoyable social occasion. Those who do not have any sense of any of those needs, and it is not always easy to see why they should.

Unless it is fear: fear of future redundancy, never mind its imminence, propels some towards further learning as an insurance against difficulties in the future. But surprising numbers of people behave like ostriches, almost denying to themselves that anything so drastic could apply to them.

Doubters or not, many of the deterrents which were explored earlier in this chapter concerned with the 'disenchanted' are as serious for the ranks of the missing who are employees. There are all the place, space, time and travel availability factors. But probably of more importance again are questions about the curriculum on offer. If courses seem neither appealing nor interesting there is no reason why any doubter could be enticed into signing up, or to begin to climb over the threatening 'fear bar'.

There is a different way of approaching this. Perhaps the largest obstacle to people continuing to learn after they leave school or enter employment is that even if their needs are not as serious as the disenchanted, the school education experience of these missing employees did little to encourage them to think of learning as anything more than being connected with income so that they had little sense that it can make life a more interesting experience altogether. This is a deep-routed obstacle to lifelong learning.

The sting in the tail of the OECD Report in 2001 of its Programme for International Student Assessment (PISA) is what it has to say about reading for pleasure. All of those 36 per cent of boys and 29 per cent of the combined figure for boys and girls cannot be located solely in any section of the population. Of course it leaves out the unknown number of those who may find themselves reading later in life, but some have to be found among the employed. If so, those figures make dismal reading for the prospects for increasing the participant rate in lifelong learning. If people do not read for pleasure, they are hardly likely to jump at the first opportunity presented for further learning. This can be an indication of how deep-rooted is the difficulty of persuading people that learning is a good thing.

However serious all these issues are in trying to understand why so many people have no sense of the value of lifelong learning, there are two other factors which can make the previous explorations seem trivial: adult growth and development; and top-down provision.

Adult growth and development

One of the most extraordinary characteristics of many continuing education departments and further education lecturers who teach adults is that not enough members of staff seem to have taken the trouble to try to understand the significance of the stages of life of their actual and potential students and the consequences of such understanding for their teaching. This is a mismatch of a different order, and despite the glowing references to lifelong learning as self-development in most public policy documents, it is extremely doubtful that the civil servants who draft those documents know much about it either. The professional advisers ought to know the topic backwards, but if they do there is little evidence that their expertise informs official thinking about lifelong learning.

Most discussion of lifelong learning seems to be based in part on the built-in assumption that adults are all of a kind. Everyone knows that adolescents can be difficult to deal with whether at home or in school, college or university or in work. They can be unpredictable, moody, aggressive, resentful, ungrateful, confused, impossible and a general pain, as well as generous, loving and lovable, appreciative, and a joy to have around. They can be two different people. One lives at school and in the streets and one lives at home. Adults are no different; they too can display some of these characteristics. But not enough people recognise and accept that adulthood itself is not a steady progression from post-adolescence to the grave, that for many it too has its periods of instability, inconsistency, confusion, uncertainties. It is the acceptance of this fact which ought to be a fundamental consideration underlying every attempt to formulate policies for lifelong learning.

Adolescence is not a neatly ruled-off period obeying some chronological time machine. Puberty can set in early or late. Explorations into self-discovery through trying out various forms of independence sometimes do not occur until the late teens or even into the early twenties. Others seem impatient of any whiff of parental restraint almost as soon as they enter secondary school and even earlier. The same applies to adults. Chronological age does not necessarily correlate with fairly well-defined stages of adult growth and development. And just as adolescents at the rebellious stage can be not only difficult for teachers to teach but, in strictly technical terms, they may not be able to engage because of the turbulence going on in their heads and bodies, so the same can be applied to adults. A man who is at the dependency stage of his development can be driven to distraction by problems with his mortgage when he has to make decisions, none of which are to his liking. A mother who is exasperated by the persistent demands of a pre-school child and who is at a conformist stage of development is likely to make matters worse by worrying about the way she will be seen by others if that child's behaviour erupts in public. Red-faced women with screaming children in supermarkets tell the story all too often. Some learn from those experiences; others feel defeated by them.

All this can be expressed in tabular form to indicate the complex and rich variety of combinations of tasks and capacities to undertake them which can occur at different times in adult life.

Table 5.1 Erikson's life story

Basic trust versus mistrust	Infancy	−1
Autonomy versus shame and doubt	Early childhood	2–3
Initiative versus guilt	Pre-puberty	3–6
Industry versus inferiority	Puberty	7–12 or so
Identity versus role confusion	Adolescence	12–18 or so
Intimacy versus isolation	Early adulthood	20s
Generativity versus stagnation	Middle adulthood	late 20–50
Integrity versus despair	Later adulthood	50+

Source: Erikson (1950).

In *Childhood and Society*, Erikson (1950) set out a version of adult growth and development indicating the main tensions occurring at different stages of life and the tasks associated with each of those stages. In 1959 he put those figures alongside these eight phases (Table 5.1).

It is obvious that there is no automatic movement for any individual from one phase to another, no neat transition, and that some may straddle more than one stage at once. However, as a set or reminders of the kinds of people we all are, it is helpful to think about it in relation to the missing from lifelong learning.

Another way of thinking about the same issue is to overlay those different stages of life with the day-to-day tasks associated with them. A late adolescent is likely to be more concerned with achieving emotional independence than anything else and may see choosing a particular kind of employment as a means of doing just that. His older neighbour may well be married and facing the problems of beginning to bring up a family, with all the domestic responsibilities that go with it at the same time as trying to map out a pattern for his working future while his partner has to sort out her priorities between looking after home and children while tending her own needs through some sort of work or voluntary activity outside the home. Meanwhile the neighbours on the other side who have reached the middle years of life are having to cope with the empty-nest problem of children leaving home which may coincide with difficult decisions about where to live and employment changes which are being forced upon them, or perhaps they are welcoming the prospect of retirement. Older uncles and aunts, and indeed the adolescent's parents, are having to come to terms with the biological changes which are upsetting their assumptions about what they can do, adjusting to declining strength and perhaps health, while one of the grandparents may find themselves suddenly alone when the other dies and subsequently has to find some pattern of living which is tolerable. Again, particularly in these days, there is nothing automatic about any such set of transitions. The consequences of the rapid economic and social changes that have transformed society in the past twenty-five years mean that it is just as possible for the young family man to be made redundant as the woman in later life finding employment well into her late sixties and then going into voluntary work.

The worst thing about this is when crises occur 'out of time', at an unexpected stage of life. The death or incapacitation of a spouse in a young family when everything appeared to be going smoothly; some serious ailment suddenly strikes a child; an adolescent has a fatal accident while on his beloved motorcycle; a parent dies just as a fully developed support system had been worked out for the family; unexpectedly a marriage begins to fall apart. When any of those incidents, or the myriad others which can occur to children, parents, grandparents, bursts in on a family or home when no such thing was expected, they can have a devastating effect on people's capacity to cope. Some tasks seem close to being impossible to complete.

R. Murray Thomas quoted Havighurst in his book *Human Development Theories* to spell out this approach to the human story:

> A development task is a task which arises at or about a certain period in the life of an individual, successful achievement of which leads to his (or her) happiness and to success with later tasks, while failure leads to unhappiness in the individual disappointment by society and difficulty with later tasks.
>
> (Havighurst, in Thomas 1972)

Havighurst offers six stages to cover a lifetime (Table 5.2). He comments that what goes on in any one of these periods in the first place is influenced if not determined by biological structure. This is the context for the influence brought to bear by the particular culture in which an individual is reared, the expectations in that culture about the level of task performance, and the personal values and aspirations of individuals.

As a measure of how all considerations of lifelong learning should have changed over the past twenty-five years, it is worth noting how the tasks related to those differentiated age brackets were expressed in the 1980s (Table 5.3).

Table 5.2 The six stages of a lifetime

Infancy and early childhood	0–5
Middle childhood	6–12
Adolescence	13–17
Early adulthood	18–30
Middle age	31–54
Later maturity	55 +

Source: Havighurst, in Thomas (1972).

Table 5.3 Developmental tasks for the adult years

16–25 Late adolescence	25–35 Early adulthood	35–45 Midlife transition	45–57 Middle adulthood	57–65 Late adulthood	65+ Late maturity
• Achieving emotional independence • Preparing for family life • Choosing and preparing for a career • Developing an ethical system	• Deciding on a partner • Starting a family • Managing a home • Starting an occupation • Assuming civic responsibilities	• Adapting to a changing time perspective • Revising career plans • Redefining family relationships	• Maintaining a career or developing a new one • Restabilising family relationships • Making mature civic contributions • Adjusting to biological change	• Preparing for retirement	• Adjusting to retirement • Adjusting to declining health and strength • Becoming affiliated with late adult groups • Establishing satisfactory living arrangements • Adjusting to death of spouse • Maintaining integrity

Chickering, Havighurst, Chickering Associates 1981.

Trying to construct a table to cover a lifetime of eventualities for the early twenty-first century would not only look very different but would probably be impossible in the range of cross-over ages and tasks which might be listed. So many of the age-related norms have broken down: millionaires are retiring in their thirties; midlife crises stretch into the sixties; the blurring of sex differentiations; dual-career families with both husband and wife fully employed; new forms of extended family with stepfathers, stepmothers, step- and half-brothers and sisters, new meanings for the empty-nest syndrome as roles within families shift. And all this does not take account of demography and ageing. Much of the current literature on adult growth and development pays far more attention than before to ageing in the later years, with concerns about new roles and contributions from those in their sixties, seventies and eighties. This is a measure of the changed context for thinking about LLL.

Alternatively, life can be presented with a different set of descriptions (Table 5.4).

New Passages by Gail Sheehy (1996) is an attempt to bring her *Passages* (1976) up to date to take account of all the changes which have occurred during the intervening years. She writes:

> There is a revolution in the life cycle. In the space of one short gener-ation the whole shape of the life cycle has been fundamentally altered. People today are leaving childhood earlier but they are taking longer to grow up and much longer to grow old. That shifts all the stages of adulthood – by up to ten years. A healthy woman who reaches the age of 50 can expect to see her 82nd birthday. A healthy man who reaches the age of 50 can expect to live until 77. This amounts to a second lifetime.

The participation of women in higher education is a commentary on that:

> The greatest increases among students in higher education are among women. Nearly ten times more women matriculated universi-ties part time today than 25 years ago. 90 per cent of Britain's younger generation of women aged 16–24 hold some level of qualification. By contrast nearly half the women aged 35 to 55 have no academic quali-fications. And over three quarters of women in their mid fifties have none.
>
> (Demos 2002)

Table 5.4 Some milestones of ego development

Stage	Character development	Interpersonal style	Conscious preoccupation	Cognitive style
Impulsive	Impulsive, fear of retaliation	Receiving, dependent, exploitative	Bodily feelings, especially sexual and aggressive	Stereotyping conceptual confusion
Self-protective	Fear of being caught externalising blame, opportunistic	Wary, manipulative, exploitative	Self-protective trouble, wishes advantage, control	
Conformist	Conformity to external rules, shame, guilt for breaking rules	Belonging, superficial, niceness	Appearance, social acceptability, banal feelings, behaviour adjustment, problems, reasons, opportunities	Conceptual simplicity, cliches, multiplicity
Conscientious conformist	Differentiation of norms and goals	Aware of self in relation to group, helping		
Self-aware conscientious	Self-evaluating standards, self-criticism, guilt for consequences, long-term goals and ideals	Intensive, responsible, mutual, concern for communication	Differentiated feelings, motives for behaviour, self-respect, achievements, traits, expression	Conceptual complexity, idea of patterning
Individualistic	Add respect for individuality	Add dependence as emotional problem	Add development, social problems, differentiation of inner life from outer	Add distinction of process and outcome, increased conceptual complexity, complex patterns, toleration of ambiguity, objectivity
Autonomous	Add coping with conflicting inner needs, toleration Add reconciling inner conflicts renunciation of unattainable	Add respect for autonomy, interdependence, cherishing the individual	Vividly conveyed feelings, integration of physiological, psychological causation of behaviour, role conception, self-fulfilment, self in social context, add identity	
Integrated	Add reconciling inner conflicts Renunciation of unattainable	Cherishing the individual	Add identity	

Note
Add means in addition to previous entry.

Source: Adapted from Loevinger (1976), quoted in Martineau and Chickering (1981).

Sheehy offers a revised version of ages and stages and concentrates on what she calls 'second adulthood', claiming that this is where some of the most arresting changes are taking place. As she puts it:

> People will work longer beyond 65 not only because they want a purpose in living but because they will need to be able to support themselves and others for longer.

- Provisional adulthood 18–30
- First adulthood 30–45
- Second adulthood 45–85+
- Age of mastery 45–65
- Age of integrity 65–85+.

Taking the above stages of development as the context for asking the question why are the missing missing, some answers leap off the page. It is quite obvious that someone at the conscientious stage of development is well placed not only to participate in further learning but is also likely to want to do so either for the satisfaction of learning more or because of the need to do so in order to stay in employment. Conversely, someone at an earlier stage of development, say, at the self-protective stage, is likely to find all kinds of reasons for not participating in lifelong learning despite the fact that, seen from the outside, doing so seems essential for self-preservation seen as an objective assessment of that individual's circumstances.

Adult learning

All this clearly affects the timing of the readiness of people to engage in lifelong learning, but before trying to see what that means in practice it is necessary to rehearse in parallel some comments on how adults learn. The general tendency is to assume that when adults learn, they all learn in the same way. They do not. Attentive teachers know that, and try to vary their methods of teaching accordingly. Some adults learn best by sitting quietly in a corner reading a book and making notes. Some seem able to do this with the radio playing in the background which can sound like the foreground to others. Some like nothing better than listening to what a teacher has to say, and learning that way. Still others need to be engaged in some physical activity to stir their minds into learning. And that does not mean heavy manual labour. Many a time someone will get up, walk around the room, stand looking out of a window, almost to allow the mental learning machine to freewheel for a while. Discussion is for others the best way of learning. And of course many men or women are likely to use a combination of these different means of learning.

These various ways of learning are the foundations for the work of David

Kolb. In 1976 he published a book called *Learning Styles Inventory* (Kolb 1976). He developed what he called an 'Experiential learning cycle', which articulated what he distinguished as four different modes of learning, and set them out in a logical sequence to show the relationship between each mode. He began with the proposition that some people learn best from concrete experience, from doing things. (I don't really learn from books; I'm much better at doing things than learning from them.) Next he pointed out that some learn best from observation and reflection. (I can sit and read and really take it in, but when it comes to doing something with my hands I am useless.) Others find that abstractions, generalisations and concepts are their preferred way of learning. (I like to know what the latest research has to say about the topic.) Still others learn most from testing a concept, proposition, principle, by trying it out in different situations. (I don't really know how I sorted that out; trial and error I suppose.)

So Kolb set out these four different approaches to learning and showed their relationship in a cyclical sequence. Concrete experience provides the basis for observation and reflection. Observation and reflection are assimilated into what is already known and provide a new conceptual map for action. That new action produces new experiences and so the sequence begins all over again. He says:

> The effective learner relies on four different learning modes – CON-CRETE EXPERIENCE (CE), REFLECTIVE OBSERVATION (RO), ABSTRACT CONCEPTUALISATION (AC) AND ACTIVE EXPERI-MENTATION (AE). That is he must be able to involve himself in new experiences fully, openly and without bias in new experiences (CE), he must be able to reflect on and observe that experience from many different perspectives (RO). He must be able to create new concepts that integrate his observations into logically sound theories (AC), and he must be able to use these theories to make decisions and solve problems (AE).

Kolb is not saying that people learn in only one way. He is asserting that a combination of those ways leads to truly effective learning, and there is no rule which says that everyone begins the learning cycle at the same point. Some begin with books and some with doing things, but whatever mode is preferred it is neither more nor less important than the others.

These ideas are expressed differently by Henry and Mumford in their *Manual of Learning Styles* (1992). They organise the learning cycle as:

- *Activity:* Doing something.
- *Reflection:* Thinking about experience.
- *Theory:* Seeing where it fits in with theoretical ideas.
- *Pragmatic:* Applying knowledge to actual problems.

Table 5.5 Likes and dislikes

Style	Likes	Dislikes
Activity	Doing, experiencing, enjoys games, practical activities, anything which is energetic.	Sitting around, working alone, theorising, having to listen to others droning on.
Reflection	Time to think, observe, take it all in first, love to watch others, needs some solitude, above all time.	Being hurled into activity, having no time to think, crammed timetables, lack of privacy, no time to prepare.
Theorists	To know where something fits into overall ideas and concepts, analyses and logic, being overstretched, abstract concepts, structures and clarity.	Frivolity, mindless fun, wasting time, not being able to question and be sceptical, lack of timetable and proper structure.
Pragmatists	Practical problem-solving, relevance to 'real' world, learning that answers the question: How to apply this?	Anything airy-fairy, learning that makes too many references to past or future and attention to *now*

Source: Rogers (2001: 24).

This is worked out more fully by Jenny Rogers in the fourth edition of her *Adult Learning* (Rogers 2001: 24) in terms of likes and dislikes (Table 5.5).

As with the stages of adult growth and development, to ask the question why are the missing missing against that analysis of the various ways in which different people learn is to find some obvious answers. If an individual joins in a learning opportunity offered in a mode which does not accord with his or her preferred way of learning, then it may turn out to be a not very satisfying experience. There is little point in expecting a skilled machine-tool craftsman who has been made redundant to be enthusiastic about a retraining course which purports to make him employable as a stores assistant by equipping him with the principles of stocking inventories and legal regulations if he has no aptitude for learning from books. He would be better off spending the time shadowing a stores assistant, watching what he does, noticing the order in which he does things, and making some notes afterwards to remind himself of what he had learned: CE and RO. Or his discomfort at trying to learn independently may make it very hard indeed for him to complete the spreadsheet assignment as part of learning how to compose a business plan for establishing his own small business. Similarly, if a woman who has been caught up in a 'downsizing' programme which results in her job as a clerical assistant disappearing, one in which she was perfectly happy getting on with whatever assignments she was given to do as long as she was left alone to get on with it, looks through advertisements and sees vacancies as a shop assistant, the likelihood is that she would hate it. A retraining course which concentrated on customer care and relations (CE and RO) so that she could cope with all and sundry and which required her to have some work experience as part of the course could be a disaster, because about the last thing she would feel happy doing is dealing with unpredictable situations (AE).

Conversely, some very clever people can become more effective learners if they are required to undertake some practical experience alongside their formal study through books. There is a medical programme for preparing doctors in MacMaster University in Canada where the first thing which happens to new students is that they are shown a patient and told to find out what the problem is. The assumption here is that learning from books is what they are familiar with and are good at (AC), so learning through doing something (CE) will probably be new to them as a way of learning academically (RO), expand their repertoire of approaches to learning and prepare them for trying out what they have found on a different patient (AE).

As well as having vital cognitive significance in describing the different ways in which people learn, this cycle has great psychological importance. One of the most important aspects of learning for individuals is the personal satisfaction which comes from a sense of achievement at having completed a learning task successfully. The implication of the four learning modes is that asking someone to engage in a learning task through using a learning mode which does not fit with their preferred way of learning runs the risk of making that task unnecessarily hard to accomplish as well as risking causing a sense of frustration along the way. It can be a very discouraging experience. And since encouragement is the oil which keeps the motivational thrust moving smoothly, fitting a person to the appropriate learning style becomes a central issue for considering ways of making the missing visible.

There are strong connections between these theoretical accounts of the way we are and the mismatches which help to explain why the missing are missing. The argument is based on the theoretical propositions about human growth and development and learning styles, saying essentially that curriculum and pedagogy need to move towards more individualised learning programmes and away from classroom-style provision which assumes that everyone is going to learn the same way.

It is not only theory. A survey conducted for the National Institute for Adult Continuing Education by Professor Field, as reported in the *THES* issue of 17 May 2002, noted that the proportion of lifelong learners in the population is higher among those who are separated or divorced. He said, 'Perhaps it is to do with flexibility and adaptability. People who enjoy learning for its own sake may also be people who enjoy the challenges of change much more, and are much less frightened by the prospect of breaking up ... people who regularly go out with family and friends are almost twice as likely to be lifelong learners.' Turn that on its head for the missing, and some practical, penetrating pedagogical issues arise.

There is another strand to the argument which makes the same point but from a different perspective.

Top-down micro-management

This strand is the top-down characteristic which describes the government's approach to the vast majority of what is offered currently to the missing as lifelong learning. Look in any catalogue or brochure of a further education college and there are impressive lists of courses under the lifelong learning heading. Were you to ask how many of those courses actually recruited students and ran, the answer might not be as impressive. There are technical reasons for that which are concerned with regulations for funding, but that is not the point for this argument. The point is that under current top-down regulations, with the best will in the world it is well-nigh impossible for colleges to take full account of what the missing might want to learn even if they were aware of the opportunity. Add in all the previous difficulties experienced by formal education institutions in attempting to attract the missing – place, appearance, formalities – and it is hardly surprising that if what is on offer does not fit with the circumstances of potential students they do not show up.

The worrying aspect to this is that in the government's White Papers and commissioned reports, the top-down provision seems to dominate the approach to lifelong learning. It is true that there is a stark and encouraging contrast between the rather narrow instrumental emphasis the Tories gave in the early 1990s on personal competitiveness to serve national economic interests, and the current inventive, assertive attitude in the learning age which put a powerful imprimatur on learning as an essential element in fulfilled living. But the tendency remained to assume, almost automatically, that it was the formal which lay at the heart of thinking about lifelong learning. And that led inexorably to the continuance of the emphasis on top-down provision.

For all its splendid championing of further education for the huge contribution it can make to society through lifelong learning, *The Kennedy Report* hardly gets outside the formal provision. So when its clarion call goes up to challenge the instrumental, there is no hint about using another route:

> Prosperity depends on a vibrant economy, but an economy that regards its own success as the highest good is a dangerous one. In a social landscape where there is a growing gap between those who have and those who do not have, the importance of social cohesion cannot be ignored.
> (DfEE 1997b)

Little attention seems to be paid to the potential mismatch implications of provision in formal institutions.

The same is true of Dearing. According to that report a Learning Society is one:

> in which people in all walks of life recognise the need to continue in education and training throughout their working lives and who see learning as enhancing the quality of life throughout its stages.
>
> (DfEE 1997a)

This seems to return to lifelong learning as a way for individuals to improve their working performance to sustain a competitive economy, with the implication that institutions' business is to ensure that this occurs. Command performance again. It almost echoes a DfEE pamphlet, *Learning to Compete: Education and Training for 14–19* (DfEE 1996):

> Investment in learning in the 21st century is the equivalent to investment in the machinery and technical innovations that were essential to the first industrial revolution. Then it was capital. Now it is human capital.

The top-down approach is seen clearly in the use of language. Both reports talk about a return to learning as if formal education was the place to return to, assuming that it was something which people had actually left. You cannot return to a place where you have not been. This is half the problem. A large proportion of the missing have never been in formal education in any engaged way beyond early adolescence. Physically they may have been present; mentally they were somewhere else. Mismatches all round.

This top-down approach to attempting to increase the number of people who continue to learn throughout their lives is heavily emphasised through the Learning and Skills Act which set up the Learning and Skills Council. It shows the same tension as in *The Kennedy Report*. In his introduction to *Learning to Succeed: A New Framework for Post-16+ Learning* (DfEE 1999), David Blunkett said:

> Lifelong learning ... will ensure the means by which our economy can make a successful transition from the industries and services of the past to the knowledge and information society of the future and will also contribute to sustaining a civilised and cohesive society in which generational disadvantages can be overcome.

How is this to be done? By having a Learning and Skills Council which is responsible for all 16+ provision whether in schools or further education colleges and up to the grave. This is centralising with a top-down provision with a vengeance. And with that centralisation goes the micro-management from the centre through the funding systems. Unless someone, somewhere, promotes a visionary path of development for the LSC, it is likely all the mismatches which keep the missing missing will be left untouched and perhaps even go unrecognised.

Lurking in the undergrowth beyond the reach of current schemes for lifelong learning lies an awful warning which Sheehy issues:

> The gap between the professional class and the poor seems to be widening inexorably. There is a whole new class of men lacking the skills and education to work in the post modern economy who may never be able adequately to support a family and direct their own lives. And a woman living on a council estate in the northeast of England probably has a life expectancy not much better than a century ago. Nevertheless the more fortunate in society will increasingly be faced with a new timetable of adult life.
>
> (Sheehy 1996)

Almost brutally, that poses the mismatch problem for lifelong learning.

Chapter 6

Towards wider participation

Encouraging it

There is little hope of success in re-tuning lifelong learning to encourage wider participation without some fundamental rethink of the implications of what it is and what it is for and why it is so important. This goes back to rediscovery, with all the pointers for direction it suggests need following. That rethink needs to be undertaken in three areas in particular. Two are the direct responsibility of government: top-down centralisation and the obsession with the vocational with formal accredited qualifications as an economic booster. The third runs far wider than government: it concerns the health of democracy itself. Taken together they mean asking awkward questions about how to correct the comprehensive mismatch which seems to characterise lifelong learning at present.

However, there is a fourth area: the staffing of lifelong learning. That too raises contentious questions about pay and conditions of service, for there is an uneasy relationship between current arrangements and contemporary requirements.

Centralisation/decentralisation

There are two points to make about centralisation. The first is that since 1979 all governments have spoken about it with forked tongues. They say they want to hand power back to the people. They act by taking more and more power and responsibility from local authorities. The second is that centralisation tends to throttle innovation. Decentralising is essential to pave the way to the deinstitutionalisation of the current provision of lifelong learning, namely to enable it to do its work. There is a good deal else as well, but that is for another story.

In 1997 *The Times Educational Supplement* carried an article under the heading of 'Guru predicts classroom exodus'. Quoting Professor David Hargreaves who was then, as now, a special adviser to the government, it read:

> Indeed unless we dismantle and reconstruct many social institutions including education, conceptions 'the learning society' or 'lifelong learning' will remain pure rhetoric. The traditional education system must be replaced by polymorphic education provision with an infinite variety of multiple forms of teaching and learning.

Just so. The headline may be catching, but it suggests the wrong story. What Hargreaves was implying was that the current system just does not engage with up to about 50 per cent of those it seeks to serve under the label of lifelong learning. And it is these non-participants to which the government refers when from the Prime Minister down it worries that the country lags so far behind the levels of skills available in other countries, with the result that the health of the economy is threatened. Sometimes there is almost a plaintive note in these official comments as if it is someone else's fault. But it is the government's own policies which are at fault in not coming to terms with the problem of how to make the best contribution to those caught on the wrong side of the widening gap. At present all groups are covered for lifelong learning in theory, even the poor. The government is entitled to say in effect that we are doing all we can. In a sense it is trying to do too much, and the problem is that the doing begins in the wrong place, with such frightening implications. If we need polymorphic institutions they cannot be created by regulation.

Professor Frank Coffield of Newcastle University put it differently at a conference on 7 May 2002 (*THES*, 10 May 2002) in the Institute of Education in London:

> As jobs become more complex and skilled, they are likely to require more discretion to carry them out, but instead of trusting individuals to monitor their own performance, government policies are predicated on a deep lack of trust in professionals.

That is the price of over-centralisation; a poor way of getting the best service when and where it is required.

Decentralisation/centralisation

Put the other way around, when decentralisation comes first, what would dismantling and reconstructing mean in practice? The government getting out of the way: that is the first prerequisite for re-tuning lifelong learning.

At one level this is not as dramatic as it sounds. Local authorities need to be brought back into the arena as major players. One of the most serious political issues is the castration of local government. This is not just a matter of structure. As local government has had increasingly less control over what it is supposed to be responsible for, since it acts under instructions from central government, so its overall significance for people in local areas has declined. As a result there are fewer and fewer chances of recruiting people of high quality as candidates for elections. Successful men and women in any walk of life have no interest in serving on committees which have little or no executive power. For lifelong learning it is no surprise that the token representation on the Training and Enterprise Councils has not filled local authorities with great excitement about promoting it, let alone playing key roles in developing the local economies. Perhaps their role in relation to the LSC will change all that, but if given their heads there can be little doubt that LEAs could make a huge contribution to the general development of lifelong learning. The key however is 'if given their heads'. This means re-empowering local government, loosening the shackles which currently chain it to the centre.

A review commissioned by the Department for Transport, Local Government and the Regions and submitted in May 2002 points the finger: 'The government's concentration on micro-performance management is seen in many localities as a distraction. There are frustrations over the centre's unwillingness to allow experimentation and its desire to dictate means as well as ends.' It went over the ground citing micro-management, repetitive interference and lack of co-ordination between Whitehall departments. It offered a damning analysis. Any reasonable person would conclude that that is the last way to try to enlist local government in the drive to develop lifelong learning.

The voluntary organisations too have so much to teach the formal system, and this should be used more extensively. The simple lesson they have to offer is that the formal system does not have to be experienced formally. Members of the WEA meet where they want to meet and often that means in one another's homes. So do members of the U3A. As soon as there is talk about meeting where people want to meet so that they can learning something they want to learn, all the social aspects of people meeting in groups come to bear. And, since lack of coherence is such a prominent characteristic of our increasingly fragmented society, few things are more important than encouraging people to get together for a common purpose. There is no reason why a sense of common purpose should not emerge for groups through lifelong learning.

The voluntaries point to something else. Environmentalists have helped develop the understanding that place matters. It matters just as much in public policy as in private life. It matters for the poor as well as the rich. Any employee will say that working in an agreeable place can transform attitudes to their work as well as towards other people there. Setting out each morning to go to a place which is pleasing in its own right is as important as going back to a welcoming home. Architecture, colour and furniture all play their part, and that part need not be expensive either. With less centralisation, local and voluntary organisations could get on with tilling the ground in preparation for wider participation, developing lifelong learning in the light of what they consider to be best for the local circumstances. Government departments and the LSC will say that they do this already. Whatever they may think, anyone working in lifelong learning knows better. Regulations strangle initiative. But if the voluntary bodies can make a success of working within the regulations which affect them, why can the formal system not do the same?

The short answer is that the heavy centralisation which has characterised the government's approach to education over the past twenty-five years works against those who try to be imaginative within the present regulations. The longer answer takes longer to tell.

Initiative debased

In retrospect, one of the more intriguing aspects of the hugely successful expansion of school building in the 1950s and 1960s is the way that demography seemed to be ignored. Very large numbers of those schools were built on housing estates created by local authorities both to improve the housing stock they had at their disposal and to accommodate the increasing numbers of people needing houses as the population grew. As housing estates grew, so did the numbers of children needing to go to both primary and secondary schools. In many places newly built schools soon ran out of space as more children came along. New buildings were added or Nisson huts were put up as temporary measures. But then as the children became young people who finished at secondary school and left home, some schools had more space than they could use. In time as resources got more and more pinched some schools were closed, amalgamated, even sold off. It was as if planners forgot that children become young people who move away from home, or if they remembered they had no contingency plans for coping with surplus accommodation.

This policy was based on a fixation with purpose-built buildings. Government building regulations specified everything from amounts of space per pupil, numbers of lavatories through to size of hall and, for secondary schools, gymnasium. All this was admirable. It produced schools the like of which had never been seen before. Light and airy, they were a joy to work in and, where they were well maintained, there is no doubt that they had a profound influence on the attitudes and behaviour of many of their pupils. Everything else was seen as second rate, though it was remarkable how with careful attention some of those second-rate buildings became first-rate education facilities.

But why was it that apparently no one thought of other ways of providing for schools expansion without the capital investment required and the subsequent embarrassment of having too many of them? Take a couple of nearby council houses, knock a few internal walls down if necessary, fix them up with all the essentials, make the necessary insurance arrangements, and there would have been a usable facility which could have been returned to its original housing purpose when the numbers of pupils declined. Scores of objections can be made to such an idea, but it is relevant to lifelong learning today.

Nowadays on the one hand there are so many people, and alarmingly large numbers of adolescents, who do not like formal institutions. On the other hand we go on building them. Further education colleges acquired extensive responsibilities for lifelong learning even though they were built for no such purpose. All over the country there are now capital building programmes to expand and/or replace old buildings with new. The question is whether it would not be more encouraging for non-participants in lifelong learning to be invited to go somewhere more familiar. Voluntary organisations can do it. Why cannot formally established education institutions do it? It returns to the point that lifelong learning which is provided through the formal system does not necessarily need to take place in formal institutions.

In the 1950s and 1960s, had a local education authority wanted to use a couple of council houses as temporary accommodation for an overflowing school it probably could have done so. The DES would have taken some persuading. Local HMI would have been involved. It would have been a contentious issue within the LEA. Chairmen and chief officers of housing and education would have had some hectic discussions. But in all probability it could have done what it wanted. Its most convincing case would have been that it knew better than central government how best to cope with tricky questions which might turn out to be temporary, and it reduced costs on the capital building account.

And now? Because of the devolution of resources from LEAs to schools and further education colleges and their governing bodies, any such initiative would have to come from them. That might suggest that there was more scope for local initiatives. In fact there is little room for local manoeuvre. An LEA would be nonplussed at any such suggestion. Its own stock of housing is so reduced by the selling off of council houses that even if it wanted to follow such an idea, politically it would be impossible. Its responsibilities have been so curtailed that it is doubtful it would know how to respond. Apart from a flat rejection it is not easy to see how the DfES could cope. Ofsted might be hauled in to go through the proposal and raise objections about the problems of ensuring the quality of the education offered. All the usual objections about health and safety and insurance would be cited as reasons for rejection. So the school might be left to linger in limbo in the capital building programme while its application lists land both it and the LEA with exhausting appeal procedures from parents who have challenged decisions about admission. Today, senior staff in hundreds of schools are currently in this position, spending long hours in the summer attending appeal hearings about admissions conducted by the LEA when they ought to be either on holiday or laying plans for developments in the coming year. Or a college knows what off-campus programmes it wants to develop but it is hampered by building and planning and spending regulations. This thinking could open the way for 'polymorphic education provision with an infinite variety of multiple forms of teaching and learning'.

This is not to suggest that decentralisation is a magic wand to deal with overcrowding, or to imply that it would lead automatically to the re-tuning of lifelong learning. It is to point to the difficulties confronted by knowledgeable and responsible people who want nothing more than freedom to make the best of their particular circumstances which they know better than any other.

It is also saying that there is a stark contrast between the devolution which has enabled Scotland, Northern Ireland and Wales to make arrangements for education, judged to suit them best, and the continuing arrangements in England, where heavy centralisation over all aspects of education remains the rule, despite the responsibilities which have been handed down to governing bodies of schools and colleges. Such a heavy hand stifles initiative. Whether it is the Higher Education Funding Council, the Learning and Skills Council or the DfES itself, regulations and requirements are in danger of turning professionals into technicians who have to follow instructions. In many cases too this is made worse by developmental programmes of one kind or another which have short-term ring-fenced money attached to them. This makes long-term planning almost impossible. What is so extraordinary about many of these schemes is that in times past the activities they set out to promote were seen as part of the normal work of people fulfilling their professional responsibilities. It seems like another version of putting a price ticket on things which are now somehow additional but ought to be seen as integral parts of a normal whole.

Professionals demeaned

This tendency for the government's direct interventions to reduce the professionalism of professionals has reached very serious levels. More and more men and women in all forms of public service are required to comply with instructions for ever more complicated and detailed forms to be returned so that all activities are monitored, reported and can be policed. In effect this dictates over wide areas of the work of public servants, what they do on a day-to-day basis. This is not only an issue for education and so for lifelong learning within it. In every other public service regulations have poured forth from Whitehall. There can be no denying that governments need to find ways of effecting reforms to improve public services and to have mechanisms to scrutinise implementation. It is just that over-centralisation is not the wisest way of seeking such reforms, especially when the effect is to make professionals feel demeaned and not trusted to do their jobs properly. Add the continual frustration at spending time on paperwork instead of attending to their central professional responsibilities and it is not surprising that so many professionals feel resentful.

Commenting on this state of affairs in his book Liberal Anxieties and *Liberal Education: What is Education Really For and Why it Matters* (1999: 90), Alan Ryan, Warden of New College, Oxford observes that the core problem lies in reconciling education for life in a free and complex society with fundamental rights and liberties of individual citizens that are the defining characteristics of such a society. And 'education and schools are governed by DfEE circulars in a way no American would think a free society could tolerate'.

Devolution

So how and where could such deinstitutionalisation be brought about? The first place to look is at central government. There is a Minister for Lifelong Learning. That Minister is part of the ministerial team at the DfES. There have been a succession of government Green and White Papers which in part focus on means of making more headway with participation rates for lifelong learning. A great deal of energy and resources have gone into those efforts. But what next, since so far it all has produced such disappointing results?

One idea might be to transfer lifelong learning to another government department which appears to have closer relationships than the DfES itself, with the missing participants grouped together, as mentioned earlier. But quite apart from the huge problems of effecting such a transfer, and the awkward division of labour it implies, there is no other suitable department which could be relied on to do any better. The Home Office's record of education in the Prison Service hardly shows the kind of humane approach which is necessary. Social Services have enough to be going on with. Even by default the DfES seems the most likely body to try something else. There is of course the Social Inclusion Unit which at first sight looks like a natural home for LLL for the groups listed earlier. Just the mention of it conjures up a battlefield with civil servants running up and down Whitehall as departments seek to cement their positions in resistance to joined-up government. To bring it off successfully would need someone of towering authority with the energy to realise a vision which might lie behind it. Such people seem in short supply.

There is a more obvious and immediate way of reconstructing and deinstitutionalising. It is called devolution. The government is ambiguous about devolution. It was as good as its word in establishing a Parliament in Scotland and an Assembly in Wales. But for England increased control from the centre in every public service has galloped apace. There is an understandable urge to try to promote from the centre for a government which is anxious to reform those services and to show that tax money delivers better services, and so retain its reputation for prudence. It is also understandable that in its exasperation that things do not change as fast as it wants, direction from the centre looks to be one of the few ways of trying to move in a hurry. However, impatience seems to have become instruction.

That exasperation is a long-standing story. Frustration that central government was unable to ensure that money was spent by local authorities as it intended on further education boiled over in the 1970s. The Manpower Services Commission was invented as a device to enable central government to ensure that large sums of money which heretofore had been allocated to local authorities were actually spent on further education in ways which central government wished. Earlier, Shirley Williams had issued her thirteen points for universities to respond to, realising that there was trouble ahead. They ignored them. This has led inexorably to the current heavy centralisation not only of their funding but of the scrutiny of academic work and all that goes with it. So the centralising tendency was there long ago. No doubt ministers and their senior civil servants have a taste for it too. All this is understandable. At that time devolution had entered the political vocabulary but nothing came of it for many years. In any case central government was not trying to micro-manage institutional change through its policies; it was trying to change curricula so that it was in tune with the world in which it was developing.

What is not so easily understandable as a serious attempt to effect long-standing institutional change is for the government to ignore everything that is known about institutional change. League tables and information papers of everything under the sun can appear to effect change, but much of it is superficial, a quick fix. Evolution or revolution are always contrasting approaches to institutional change. The government risks falling into the revolutionary trap. Revolutions never produce what they were intended to produce. Evolution is slow but it can be steady. Impatience needs curbing to nurture it, and the vital element about it is that it can then be based on the people who are actually doing the job which needs reform, however difficult those people may be. Unfortunately centralisation not only stifles local initiatives; it also leads to disaffected people. Thus however well intentioned, micro-management from the centre is likely to be self-defeating. It tends to leave professionals feeling on the periphery of their work when success depends on their being fully engaged.

From some points of view the arrogance of central government is unbelievable. To follow perfectly acceptable policy developments with detailed requirements for implementation seems crass. No matter how carefully and thoroughly ministers may consult, however many senior civil servants are sent out on secondment to experience temporarily for themselves the real world of doing things, it is perfectly obvious that what may work well in Land's End or Whitby is unlikely to work well in central Manchester, Birmingham or London. The government's role is not and cannot be successful in overseeing day-to-day activities and policing them using a variety of devices to ensure compliance. It may not be intentional, but that is how centralisation is experienced in education institutions of all kinds, and others for that matter. In its admirable drive to raise standards it seems to have forgotten that there are limits to government by fiat. Moreover, it is debatable how competent are civil servants to design all the kinds of procedures which lead to detailed supervision and how far ministers understand the consequences of what they approve.

What is more, centralisation runs against what appears to be the long-term development of how lives are lived. Increasing individualisation of every aspect of life is unlikely to be reversed, unless there is some severe rupturing of society. Persisting with centralisation bids fair to create a different form of frustration for government. As more and more people go their own ways, the institutions which are supposed to be serving them will be like beached whales unless they are free to swim with the tide running through their locality.

The following saying should be hung around ministers' and senior civil servants' necks: 'Give me the strength to do what I can do, the ability to see what I cannot do and the wisdom to know the difference between them.' Too often the latter is what seems to be missing.

If lifelong learning is going to flourish in the ways which are hoped for, central government has to begin to get out of the way and leave time and space for local initiatives and understandings to be put to the service locally. This applies particularly to financial regulations but in every other area of policy. It has to move back towards the position where there is public recognition that professionals are to be trusted to do their jobs professionally.

Professionals as suspects

A culture of suspicion is where Onora O'Neill, Principal of Girton College Cambridge, placed the question of trust in her May 2002 Reith Lectures (O'Neill 2002). She pointed out how curious it is that what seems to be a withdrawal of trust when dealing with professionals at one level, becomes implicit trust at another when in an emergency either a doctor or a policeman is consulted. Hence her use of 'a culture of suspicion' as a pointer to accounting for that difference. She made it clear through extensive exploration that what this means in practice in different contexts is that the present plethora of devices used by the government to monitor performances – accountability, control and audit – is based on suspicion and goes a long way towards accounting for the feeling among many professionals that they are no longer valued, let alone trusted. It also encourages the nastiness of a blaming culture. She located all these tensions in an overuse of central planning, and she pleaded for an intelligent accountability regime and an end to fantasies of exactitude based on bean counting.

As if to underline her standpoint, soon after the General Medical Association is reported in the *Independent* newspaper of 10 May 2002 as referring to its anxieties about being blamed for failing to meet government targets which are attached to the huge increase of funding for the National Health Service. Its chairman Dr Bogle said, 'It is not helpful to have the government perpetually giving targets to itself and the health professionals. Professionals are sick to death of being shackled in this way and having clinical priorities altered by government targets.' Decoded, this means: would government kindly stop its attempts at micro-management and get out of the way to let us get on with our job. By extension it also means that some form of trust needs to be reinstated. The headline read, 'Doctors say the NHS is facing its last chance.' That was because Dr Bogle also said, 'We have got to make this work or the health service which at one stage was the best in the world, may not exist.' This may not be a threat; it may even be rhetoric. It has to be someone committed professionally to the NHS. But it does put a premium on trust within the intelligent accountability systems for which Onora O'Neill was pleading. It is an urgent commitment by a key professional.

Fortuitously, the combination of an academic, Onora O'Neill, giving her Reith Lectures and the statement from practitioners by the chairman of the BMA neatly draws attention to the sense of a withdrawal of trust that has tended to undermine professionals and lies at the heart of the problems facing the government in attempting to reform public services to improve what they offer to the public. There is a particular point to make about it as it affects those men and women who are expected to promote lifelong learning along the lines expected by government. The question is: Is the government listening?

Risk aversion/risk acceptance

The relative failure so far of schemes to increase participation in lifelong learning suggests that improvements will come essentially from developing other approaches. This implies that individual professionals employed to work in lifelong learning need to be free to try whatever they think may work. Their inventiveness means they will be types of entrepreneur. Now the characteristic of entrepreneurs is that they take risks. Taking risks means that with the best will in the world there is no way of guaranteeing success in whatever enterprise it is. Risk in the business world means that a high proportion of new businesses flop. In education it is no different. Every time a member of staff goes into the field, to a housing estate, a health centre, a benefit office, a prison, seeking people where they are, in an attempt to engage people in lifelong learning who would go nowhere near a formal institution, he or she is taking huge risks. Risks mean developing schemes which may fail, however carefully they have been planned. Many may appear to be wasted. Risks have to be paid for, and this is where trust becomes a vital ingredient in seeking improvements.

The government has got itself into the foolish position of acting in a risk aversion mode. It talks about the need for enterprise. In education, as in other public service fields, it then prevents people from being enterprising. By requiring specified results before any work has been done as a condition of approving an innovative initiative and then imposing financial punishments if those results are not meet, implying it is tacitly that the government, which means civil servants, knows better than the people who actually do the work.

Professionals cannot be expected to be entrepreneurs if they are required not only to predict the numbers of people who will be involved in whatever scheme it is, but have to do their work under the threat of having funds taken away from them if those numbers are not met. Whatever the area of education, this detailed counting approach to funding is interpreted by the people doing the work as demeaning their professionalism: doubly so. The system almost invites fiddling the books of numbers, which is a professional affront, and this underlines the frustration of knowing that they are not trusted. They then tend to scoff at the very idea of civil servants and political advisers to ministers presuming to think that results can be predicted before activities begin and, even worse, that they know how to do it. Some will fantasise about applying the same criteria to the work of civil servants and politicians, thinking with glee of the prospect of their being sacked for incompetence as they failed to meet their own criteria. But they are corralled in the current heavily centralised system from which there is no escape . . . so far.

Backing risks means trusting the people taking the risks to do their best and not being surprised at failures. Failures are part of the business of achieving success. In any case, a failure is not necessarily a failure in the round. Lessons may be learned from apparent failures which may not come from apparent success.

All this and a great deal more is what it means for the government to draw back from over-centralisation, to get out of the way and see its job as creating the conditions in which new approaches to lifelong learning may be developed, and to forget about detailed monitoring of what these professionals are doing. Proper scrutiny of the use of public funds must have systems. Part of decentralisation is reforming the systems for carrying out that scrutiny.

Micro-management

Micro-management is an essential element in setting the context for encouraging wider participation in lifelong learning. More than that, it bears directly on anxieties about the low state of participation in democratic government procedures. If professionals do not feel that they are valued, what chance is there for wider participation in lifelong learning to create a greater sense of more people feeling valued? People who do not feel that they are valued have little incentive to think that politics has anything to offer them, so their votes stay unused. As *Creating Learning Cultures* puts it:

> Government's role is not to invent and pay for the whole of a comprehensive system of lifelong learning but to monitor and steer developments and re-distribute resources so that opportunities are equitable, systematic, flexible and efficient.
>
> (NAGCELL 1999: 3.17)

This centralisation and top-down approach which has now reached insidious levels connects directly with another aspect of the government's concern about lifelong learning: the economy. This was explored as an evolutionary element in the development of lifelong learning. Now it needs to be tackled at source as a major misunderstanding of the purpose and nature of lifelong learning in a contemporary technological society. What is it, and what is it for?

Vocational obsession

If the centralising tendency to control by funding is one area which needs reforming, and if lifelong learning is to be encouraged at all, then the second area is the centralising tendency to use lifelong learning as an engine to fuel the economy. It is perfectly understandable that governments should do everything possible to strengthen the economy. Indeed were they not to do so properly they could be accused of dereliction of duty. The difficulty is that society and the economy change faster and less predictably than can be matched by forms of government intervention undertaken either for planning, manpower (more or less discredited) or skills development (dicey). In some ways interventions are bound to be out of kilter. In any case, too great a concentration on vocational education and training tied to formal qualifications may not be the best way to support the economy.

One of the reasons for the relative failure of the National Council for Vocational Qualifications was just that. As fast as a group of employers tried to set down skills requirements at different levels of application for a particular industry or occupation, the danger was that they would be out of the date by the time they had been put into circulation for colleges and trainers to implement because the industry or occupation had moved on. Whether it is information technology, hotel catering and management, or decorating, painting and plumbing, or car maintenance, the same is more or less true, let alone what is required from people in manufacturing. Of course technical skills are at a premium, but employers on all sides say that what they want are men and women who can work in teams, have the ability to communicate by computer, orally and by text, and to spot and deal with problems and, above all, to have an ability to learn. A combination of qualities such as these means employers would have employees who are not set in their ways and can respond with some flexibility to whatever new circumstances lie ahead. In other words, those abilities mean that people are primed to learn more about technological and other skills rather than having them already. This can be a better way of achieving higher levels in those skills than targeting them directly.

These are not capabilities which can be reduced easily to a set of competences which may be assessed on a yes/no system. There are courses which attempt, sometimes successfully, to inculcate some of those capacities, but there is no evidence to show that they are best developed through sharp focus on a vocational description of occupational requirements. No discipline or study area has a monopoly of helping people to learn to think and none are entirely without it.

It has always been the case that much of higher education is vocational. In its earliest years the church, law, the aristocracy, all saw university education as a route to influential professional positions. Now in most higher education institutions professional and vocationally orientated courses feature prominently, and in some they outnumber all the others. Frequently tutors use team and collaborative work, projects, problem-solving and field investigations as normal parts of day-to-day pedagogy. The same is true of courses which are not designed as preparation for a profession. Learning and teaching have moved on from the stereotype of didactic performance which was assumed not to develop those qualities which employers sought. It is debatable how far that was, let alone is, accurate today. But professional preparation courses in higher education are not so much concerned with the acquisition of narrowly described skills as developing a critical and analytical mind which can cope with the unfamiliar. Other courses make the same claim; indeed, if they were not able to do so higher education would not be worthy of its name. So there was something almost impertinent in a Secretary of State going as far as he dared in instructing universities to pay more attention to the employability of their students. It was hardly an intelligent way of encouraging anything.

Unfortunately the Secretary's intervention was potentially damaging as well. One of the inevitable anxieties arising from the movement of higher education to a mass system is about the motives of the larger numbers of students attending. In a credential age it is accepted that having a degree carries with it the chance of a better job with a better salary than not having one, so that motive is clear. But the purposes of higher education are concerned with more than that. By putting such weight on the need for universities to spend time specifically in developing the employability of their students, intentionally or not, the government was tacitly implying that that was the main purpose of higher education. And without intending it, it encouraged students to see their higher education in those limited instrumental and materialistic terms.

This has something to do with the complaint made frequently by university tutors that a disturbing proportion of students do the minimum amount of work, attend classes and seminars erratically, have little interest in what they study and seem concerned solely with ending up with a degree. Certainly student indebtedness and part-time work to help cope with it have a great deal to do with this materialistic attitude of many students, and there have always been coteries of students whose approach was just that. But these attitudes need no encouragement from outside, and it is hardly the best way to encourage them to continue learning for the rest of their lives.

Fast forward to the early or mid-career of these undergraduates and it poses the question: What kind of preparation for continuing education through lifelong learning is this?

This question can be asked in the same context of further education. Margaret Hodge, Minister for Higher and Further Education, voiced anxieties about the quality of work in the colleges. She wrote:

> four in 10 colleges need to be re-inspected in one or more curriculum areas and a majority of work based training providers are weak or unsatisfactory. One in five students drops out and when you add that to an average achievement rate which is lower than we would like it means that students have a 50/50 chance of coming away from post 16 learning without having achieved what they set out to.
>
> (*Independent*, 7 March 2002)

And she wrote this about the circumstances of four million students.

The odd point about these figures is that the article also says that 90 per cent of the teaching was judged to be satisfactory or better. One wonders how it can be that satisfactory teaching can produce such high drop-out rates. The answer has to be somewhere in the curriculum. GCSEs and AS and A levels in business studies, hotel and management and so on are clearly not appropriate for many of the drop out students. Could it be that, as with higher education, an over-emphasis on preparation for employment which neglects other areas of study is self-defeating? Moreover, what kind of an inducement is that for participating in more learning later in life?

It is not fashionable these days to talk about the purpose of higher education as being the pursuit of truth. So much emphasis is put upon the need for universities to ensure that their newly qualified graduates are fully equipped to be readily employable that it is easy to make it sound as if they are becoming factories for vocational preparation. But without that guiding principle of purpose, it is impossible to talk about the education of the whole person. Currently there are dangers of that purpose being subverted. Without putting too fine a point on it, the soul of higher education is being threatened by an obsession with its material benefits. As with so many aspects of public life, this does not imply that all is well with higher education as a service and that it has no need to change to keep in tune with the fluctuations in national life. But whatever the changes, they have to be such as to continue support and maintain the integrity of its overriding purpose: the pursuit of truth.

As Sir Howard Newby, Chief Executive of the Higher Education Funding Council, put it to vice-chancellors at the April 2002 conference 'The future of higher education – help us share it':

> But there are some themes which are less commented upon. One of the most important in my view is the increasing contribution that higher education makes to civic society. We need to remind ourselves that higher education is not simply a means to an end, but is an end in itself. We need to continue to celebrate the purposes of higher education in terms of the enlightenment it brings to spreading of civilised values and promoting social progress. Universities are important institutions which lie between the state and the individual. We should not forget that we have a key role in our communities and regions in promoting civic welfare and inculcating civic values in our students.

That puts the vocational in its proper place.

Clearly it would be foolish to try and claim that lifelong learning ought to be concerned primarily with the pursuit of truth. However, there is a reasonable case for saying that many of the problems about increasing participation in lifelong learning lie in an over-emphasis on the vocational tied to formal qualifications related to economic development. Unless the overriding purpose and conduct of lifelong learning is to contribute to the development of the whole person, there is little likelihood that the economic benefits from vocational preparation will be those which are sought. 'Man does not live by bread alone.' This is true at all levels. And it is reasonable to suspect that the low participation in lifelong learning by many of those in the missing groups is connected with this rather lopsided version which concentrates too heavily on the vocational.

Rediscovering liberal education

This line of argument suggests that if the government is to make headway in encouraging wider participation in lifelong learning, it needs to shift its focus so that something akin to liberal education features as prominently as the vocational. That means changing regulations in particular financial funding systems. More on that below.

Between the two World Wars and for a couple of decades after 1945 bodies such as the WEA and university extramural departments joined later by local authorities provided a wide scope for learning in disciplines and areas which may be grouped under liberal education. True, participation was not drawn extensively from all sections of society, although many came from what was then understood as the working class. But those classes flourished because people wanted to understand better their country, the world they lived in and their place and role in it, or just to have fun. It was not called lifelong learning then, but that was what it was. For the most part it had nothing to do with vocational preparation and everything to do with people getting more engaged with the world in which they lived. Somehow lifelong learning needs to move in that direction. If ways can be found to do so, liberal education could serve many better than the vocational.

It seems no more than common sense that people who stay away from lifelong learning as it is offered at present are likely to be more interested in their immediate surroundings and circumstances than they are in training for a job which experience leads them to suspect, cynically, either may not exist, or is just a boring way of earning money. Entrepreneurs are needed to approach lifelong learning in imaginative ways.

It can be done, as many examples will testify. One such is a project called Action Learning in the Community, undertaken by the Learning from Experience Trust, at Goldsmiths College, University of London and funded by the DfEE as was (LET 2002). The idea was to persuade men and women on any form of benefit to join in learning programmes which would lead them towards courses in higher education and wean them off the benefit habit. The problem was to find them. A graduate on the staff of the Trust, who had come to Goldsmiths as an undergraduate with a not dissimilar background, spent most of his time talking to individuals, taking them to lectures to get a feel for what higher education is like, counselling them when they were in difficulties, and being generally supportive. They came: ex-offenders, some on probation, some on the edge of crime, women running single-parent households; some had given up hope; some felt rescued; one got elected as a local councillor; some enrolled on degree and diploma courses. It can be done. It is risky. This is just a single example of what imaginative approaches to lifelong learning can do if time and space allow it.

The list of activities which were eligible for funding under the DfEE's *Community Learning Prospectus* in 1988 were pointers in the same direction. They are also examples of what needs to be the guiding principle for lifelong learning. What matters is that people learn something: it does not matter very much what. That is far more important than what they learn or how they learn it. Lifelong learning is concerned to get more people learning more. However sophisticated the design of programmes, however appealing may be their glossy advertising, whatever the rhetoric, it all boils down to that. Getting more people to learn more. So if all that is about what lifelong learning is and what it is for, what is there to say about it being so important?

Lifelong learning for democracy

Democracy; therein lies the fundamental importance of lifelong learning. It reaches behind issues of attempted micro-management and vocational preparation. In the context of higher education this is what Sir Howard Newby referred to as civic values. There has to be a connection between levels of participation in lifelong learning and concerns about the poor turnout for elections at both local and central government level. By extension this questions the effectiveness of democracy itself in our society. As recorded earlier there are many references in papers issued by the DfES to lifelong learning being important in terms of citizenship and the well-being of society as a whole. Schools have been told to include citizenship in their timetables. But the importance of the connection between the two goes beyond pious references. The more people know and think they understand about the society in which they live, the more likely they are to feel they have a stake in the way they are governed, and so have some chance of influencing what happens in their own lives. This puts a premium on lifelong learning, not in some foolish idealistic way of assuming that 100 per cent participation is around the corner, but in seeking to engage as many people as possible.

At the same time that there has been a generally rising standard of living for a considerable majority of the population, there is little doubt that society has become a less kindly place. The combination of the global economy, reliance on a market economy to make the best use of resources whether public or private, and the growing individualisation of people's lives is connected with what feature in the press as stories of greed, exploitation and at worst sleaze, if not overt corruption. Of course in one form or another corporate greed has been alive and well ever since there were states and societies. But nowadays the technological possibilities of instant communication through television, the radio and the internet, all of which is echoed in the press, mean that everyone, everywhere has access to instances of personal and corporate greed. Detailed accounts of named individuals who are either directors of companies, senior executives of public services, and even vice-chancellors receiving very large increases in salaries, encourage the attitude of 'get what you can while you can'. It is worse when chairmen of failing enterprises such as Railtrack or Enron receive substantial pay-offs, or severance pay as the delicate euphemistic version puts it, as if to celebrate their failures. This all contributes to a general feeling of 'get rich if you can manage it and let the devil take the hindmost'. Cynicism abounds. Even when the benefits are thrown in of growing prosperity for so many, it is sometimes difficult to avoid fearing that society has gone sick, since there is less and less cohesion and more and more fracturing through more and more individualism. If the soul of higher education could be under threat, perhaps it is not too far-fetched to wonder if something is nagging threateningly at the soul of society itself. Certainly it is changing in ways which damage some groups of society very seriously. Lifelong learning needs to become an influence for counteracting all that.

As the American Bill Myers put it in an article entitled 'Which America will we be now', in a November 2001 issue of *The Nation*:

> The soul of democracy – the essence of the word itself – is government of, by and for the people. And the soul of democracy has been dying, drowning in a rising tide of big money contributed by a narrow unrepresentative elite, that has betrayed the faith of citizens in self government ... 'democracy will not survive if citizens turn into lemmings.'

As with other instances, in no way does this pretend that there was some glorious Golden Age in times past when everything was simpler. There was not. Now, in our highly complex society, it is hard not to hark back as if there was a Golden Age. But in many ways that is a device, unconsciously or not, for not facing up to the difficulties of our own times.

It is hard to deny that a general sense of civic responsibility has weakened. As attitudes to authority have changed, so have established structures weakened. Changes in family and domestic life, in church membership, in working lives, all militate against a sense of reliable continuity for groups of people. With more people not connected to groups as closely as before, more people are tending to look inward towards their own concerns rather than outward as members of groups are likely to do.

As individuals they find they have to do more to look after themselves. Many of the natural mechanisms for developing a civic sense have gone, as have some of the needs for it as experienced by individuals. It is in the long-term interests of the country that anything and everything that can be done is done to strengthen it again. For lifelong learning to be seen as a partner in contributing to the strengthening of a civic sense, we can invest it with a higher purpose entirely.

In part, the weakening of a civic sense must be influenced by the steady withdrawal of the state from many of the public services whether in part or in whole. The worst example is transport. It is one thing to say that individual governments have less and less influence on their own national economies as the corporate world takes on complex international operations. It is quite another for them to withdraw from some of the responsibilities for providing public services which affect the entire population and which are its direct responsibility however they are provided. When the benefits which are supposed to flow do not materialise from this withdrawal and from the combining of private business money with public funds, it is hardly surprising that large numbers feel that their votes count for little. Hordes of commuters waiting and crammed into the concourses at Waterloo and Victoria stations because of failures either by Railtrack or the train operator are unlikely to feel enthusiastic at election time. Since they believe that little notice seems to be taken of the predicament caused largely by a government in which this withdrawal has placed them, they tend to be increasingly dismissive of politicians. Train drivers, guards and station staff are no different. Most used to be proud. Now many hate to be working for a poor service. They too grow cynical about what difference politics can make to their own lives. These experiences are likely to encourage people to find ways of looking after themselves, the very antithesis of a cohesive society.

Instead of poring over the details of results of poles taken to investigate and assess the attitudes of the public to a whole range of public issues, and making deductions about policies which might attract support and which also might encourage more people to vote in parliamentary elections, all political parties should pay more attention to lifelong learning as a vehicle for reinvigorating public life. They should think about the relationships between low participation rates at elections and the 'lemmings' who stay away in droves from lifelong learning. What, they might ask, can be done about that? Can they think of ways of developing lifelong learning ideas into a programme for regeneration which looks beyond enhanced performance at work and attempts to find a better service for the missing from lifelong learning and for society as a whole? If they do that they will be asserting its important in unmistakable ways. They would be focusing on it as a public means of helping to create a society which is more kindly to more people than it is at present.

Thus the context for considering encouragement towards a wider participation in lifelong learning has three vital elements: decentralisation by government to executive authority for local action; a better balance between vocational preparation and liberal education in provision, and a need to relate participation to the wider questions about social regeneration and the effectiveness of democratic government.

Encouragement as a key

Encouragement comes at many different levels, all of which may affect the same person. It can help things along in day-to-day matters; it can open doors which formerly seemed closed; it can assist financially; it can be through companionship, sharing; it can come through some chance idea which appeared out of nowhere; it can come through a boost to self-confidence when someone makes a remark which strengthens a sense of self. Whatever it is, it is personal. And because it is personal its vital characteristic is in the response to encouragement. Encouragement has a warmth about it. It is one person responding to another, a two-way traffic. Everyone thrives on encouragement. The world can become a nicer place, less anxiety-making, when encouragement comes along. If that is true for individuals it has to be true not merely for groups of people, but throughout a population. Thus the issue for encouraging wider participation in lifelong learning is the deployment of some of those characteristics of encouragement.

The starting point for this is to remember that very large sections of population need no further encouragement to engage in any form of lifelong learning; they are doing it already. Encouragement needs to be beamed somewhere else, and that somewhere else is where the rest of the population actually is. And there is that daunting list of where some of the worst off are.

To see this in a more personal context take those groups in society which are the essential target for wider participation. In 1990 Veronica McGivney cited the following under access of education for non-participating groups:

- unskilled/semi-skilled manual workers
- unemployed
- women with dependent children
- older adults aged 50+
- ethnic minorities.

She added under basic educational needs:

- women home-makers
- people on lowest incomes, especially unemployed males

- older adults
- young adults
- 'climbers' – those who are determined to advance
- low ability.

(McGivney 1990)

This list has to be viewed against the dire comment quoted on p. 94. It is worth repeating it to set the scene.

> The gap between the professional class and the poor seems to be widening inexorably. There is a whole new class of men lacking the skills and education to work in the post modern economy who may never be able adequately to support a family and direct their own lives. And a woman living on a council estate in the northeast of England probably has a life expectancy not much better than a century ago. Nevertheless the more fortunate in society will increasingly be faced with a new timetable of adult life.

Of course there is the danger of reacting overdramatically to these sorts of prophecies in relation to lifelong learning. However true that statement may be, there needs to be a severe dose of realism. There is no conceivable reason why everyone everywhere should get enthusiastic about it, and those who for whatever reason are non-participants must be treated with the same respect as participants, however others may regret their non-participation. Even so, wider participation is by any criteria of critical importance, especially for those people who at present seem outside its reach. The task is to find ways of getting more inside its reach.

Engagement at the right place is needed to get things done, and, to be successful, engagement at the right place has to tackle all the mismatch factors outlined in Chapter 5 at all points on the compass. Whether institutionally, regulatory, physically, psychologically, pedagogically, educationally through the curriculum, engagement has to be thought through in all those respects. The government needs to work out how the discouragement which so many professionals currently experience can be turned into encouragement through celebration of successes as they occur.

For 'Only Connect' read 'Only Engage'.

Most of those whom the government and institutions are trying to include in the wider participation in lifelong learning, and which everyone agrees would be helpful, are those who simply cannot stand them. Institutions do their best but all too often they unintentionally send out all the wrong messages. Those adults resistant to anything institutional then receive messages which were sent with the very best of intentions in the wrong way.

This points to a set of areas which encouragement needs to aim at. The stakes are high for targeting them. In total those categories which McGivney cites (see pp. 114–15) have the makings of a very serious social problem, whether or not the gap referred to by Sheehy (1996) grows wider. The risks of having sizeable and perhaps increasing groups of disaffected, resentful people in a land where the vast majority of the population enjoy relative affluence hardly bears thinking about. This is quite apart from it being an ethical affront in what is supposed to be a civilised society. 'Underclass' is a term which appears less frequently than it did a decade or so ago. Perhaps it is too scary a word to use in the current political climate. 'The poor' seems to have crept into the vocabulary as a catch-all euphemism. But whether 'underclass' or 'the poor', there is no escape from the fact that McGivney's list contains a variety of categories of people who are at the bottom of the economic and social pile. Any encouragement to help them get out from underneath is only a civic responsibility, and any encouragement includes learning anything, no matter what.

Encouragement for staff

If adult learners need encouragement and support to become participants, so too do the academic and administrative staff who provide the services for them. Unfortunately all Tory moves to improve education according to their lights have brought discouragement and not encouragement to teachers in all kinds of institutions.

It begins in 1970. Margaret Thatcher had been made Secretary of State for Education and Science in Heath's Tory government. As well as earning the sobriquet of 'milk snatcher' she appointed a Committee of Inquiry under the Chairmanship of Lord James of Rusholme to consider teacher education and training. This was prompted by a belief that there were far too many teachers in training and that the system needed rationalising. One of the consequences of this rationalisation was that most of the colleges of education for training teachers were absorbed into polytechnics, and therefore came under further education regulations. The DES then applied further education regulations to all institutions conducting teacher training except in universities.

One immediate consequence of this was that the Association of Teachers in Colleges and Departments of Education found itself out on a limb. Its members were left without any institutional base for negotiating conditions of service. The decision was taken to amalgamate with the Association of Technical Training Institutions and form what is now the National Association of Teachers in Further and Higher Education (NATFHE). It was like trying to amalgamate chalk and cheese. Under FE regulations staff contracts were measured in terms of numbers of hours worked on a weekly and annual basis. In the colleges there was a completely different ethos. Hours were never discussed as a condition of employment business. There was work to be done, students to teach. The idea that lecturers' professional work could be counted on an hourly basis was anathema. It was taken as a professional insult. Not that it mattered, because the hourly regime was imposed willy-nilly.

One of the saddest consequences of this clash of cultures was that it struck a lethal blow at the concept of vocation in teaching. It begins the sorry tale of the way that increasing attempts to put a price on increasing numbers of activities undertaken by staff has contributed at all levels to their feeling driven to concentrate on pay and conditions of service which implicitly places boundaries to what professional academics do, and correspondingly what they do not do. What began as a required shift in professional behaviour of staff in colleges of education has crept through education systems of all kinds, with universities being subjected to the same kind of 'price-of-everything' mentality. Whatever else it was, the abandonment of the practice of tenure in the 1998 Act was a step in the same direction. The saddest aspect of that is that it spells out differently the contrast between trust and mistrust.

But that is where the National Association of Teachers in Further and Higher Education, the Association of University Teachers, the Professional Association, the National Union of Teachers and the Association of Women and Male Teachers currently find themselves. They argue the case with employers for their members in a bean-counting atmosphere which infects them all. Rigidity on one side tends to be reflected by rigidity on the other. When taxed with being inflexible at times when flexibility is necessary, both sides will claim that of course they recognise the need, but somehow they never get around to treating it as top priority. And it is no good the government pointing to pay advancement for excellence as if that is the issue.

The real issue is yet another example of the folly of using a one-size-fits-all approach. It does not take much thought to recognise that what may be appropriate and attractive pay and conditions contracts in Ilfracombe may be quite different from what makes sense in Tyne and Wear. So the issue then becomes devolution of a different kind. Unless heads of schools, principals of colleges and vice-chancellors are empowered to pay whatever it takes to ensure that their institutions are professionally staffed to the best level possible within the budgets available, we are faced with another chronic version of mismatch.

Sermons are not heard about facing up to the challenges of pervasive globalisation to people required to live and work in pre-globalisation conditions. If flexibility is needed to make a success of different approaches to widening participation in lifelong learning, then administrators, civil servants and politicians have a responsibility to create the conditions within which flexibility can flourish. Moreover, it will not do to blame inflexibility on unions and professional associations. It has to be the employers' side which shows some imagination. This is where encouragement would count. This is what doing it requires.

Institutions for adults

One way or another, most of the 'missing' are on some form of benefit. Just saying that conjures up all the obstacles which not only they face, but so do those who try to serve them in any attempt to move from non-participation to participation in lifelong learning. Discouragement rather then encouragement. Setting their reluctance to going anywhere near a formal education establishment alongside the relative failure of these institutions to attract people from those groups begins to question whether trying to meet their needs is more to do with local social and community services than with the national education service. No one can complain that from the Department of Education and Skills downward there has not been a long succession of efforts to provide a suitable service, yet none of them seem to have done what it was hoped they would do. Perhaps these efforts have somehow been misdirected. Perhaps they are based on practices from the past used in a very different world from that in which we live in now, rather than being based on a fundamental reassessment of what might work in the circumstances of contemporary society.

Take space as the first area. Some of the most successful initiatives to improve run-down housing estates have been where much of the planning for improvement is handed on to those who live there: delegation, in the process of which a good deal of learning went on, not that it was called that. It is impossible to join in thinking about improvements without having to recognise that some things are possible and others are impossible. That is learning. It is not too difficult to imagine that with skilful support from teachers, lecturers, anyone from the educational service, those immediate concerns about improving the general environment of a housing estate could lead to all kinds of detailed considerations: contracts and the difficulties of ensuring their fulfilment; trees and bushes and the circumstances under which they flourish; health and safety for children's playgrounds; security. Everyone will have views about all these issues. Being involved with doing something about them means that to some extent understanding the facts may modify views, and the people involved would be making it happen in their own immediate space. Lifelong learning in action.

This approach is being applied in some areas, but it needs to be a more general practice: a space within a building complex or a relatively small area; some comfortable chairs to sit in without formal rows and tables; just a nice place to be in, a normal room with people who are recognisable if not actually known.

The advantages are obvious: the place is familiar; it is practically next door. There are no transport difficulties, fewer time problems and, with luck on a reciprocal basis, baby- and childminding on hand. In such an environment it is relatively straightforward to find out what people might be interested in knowing more about. The very asking of the question sends an inviting message. Being able to ask the question and listen to answers begins to tackle at source one of the major problems of lifelong learning. If people are going to be engaged in any form of learning, it must be something they want to know rather than something other people think it would be good for them to know. If you do not ask you will never know, and if you want to harness motivation then it is silly not to ask.

This is all very different from individuals quelling their own reluctance and plucking up enough courage to go through the doors of a formal education institution. If the same question was asked there – what would you like to know more about – the pressures to answer it would be far greater. People are less likely to be tongue-tied in familiar places than in places where they are uneasy or uncomfortable.

The simple fact is that if people do not want to go to formal institutions and there is a serious policy and programme to try to encourage and engage them in lifelong learning, then engagement has to be somewhere else. And that somewhere else is where they are. It has to be. Achieving that means getting rid of some of the discouraging factors.

Indeed it is not too much to suggest that space can be a catalyst for dealing with most of the other obstacles; not all, because regulations are in a different category. Psychologically many of the obstacles are removed if getting the right space in the right place comes at the top of one's list of priorities for trying to construct appealing versions of lifelong learning. This is because most of the other obstacles are more to do with perception than with reality.

The right space in the right place avoids many of the horrors of formal institutions. An unfamiliar place is replaced by a familiar place. Anxiety at one level is reduced. Similarly the formality which inevitably goes with a formal institution is softened. For a tutor and learners to meet on the learners' own ground is to send a clear message that the power relationship between the two which tends to pertain in formal institutions is altered. It is those power relationships that act as such a severe deterrent for many. 'We' and 'them' has a chance of becoming 'us'. In these circumstances things cannot be solely on the basis of what the tutor says or wants, or what a pre-ordained programme lays out.

Pedagogy for adults

Engagement has a different connotation. It has to be worked for in ways which are subtly different from the techniques which are a classroom repertoire. Pedagogy and teaching approaches will become more learner-centred more easily than is often possible within formal institutions.

In familiar circumstances people are more ready to join in discussions so that it becomes easier to practise one of the guiding principles for adult learning – use whatever it is that learners bring with them to inform the content of the curriculum as the learning programme unfolds. In that way learners feel valued in their own right. Their self-confidence can then grow, and as it grows so can the capacity to learn, and in all probability so can the desire to learn as well, as can their understanding of what it is they really want to learn. As that begins to happen the curriculum, the content, can become a shared entity because the tutor has to figure out how best to enable participants to learn it. Perhaps the most telling aspect of all this is that the tutor has a far more enjoyable time. Where that is the case then lifelong learning has well and truly taken off. And it will have taken off for one simple reason: respect for people.

This is another way of saying that the social side of learning should never be underestimated. Meeting people who share a common purpose is something that many if not most people enjoy doing. Paying careful attention to this aspect of learning for the 'missing' is in classical terms part of a curriculum. For many present-day participants it is the social aspect of learning which appeals so strongly.

As if to underline that social aspect, Professor Field says:

> People who regularly go out with family and friends are almost twice as likely to be lifelong learners. People who enjoy gardening, rather intriguingly, are less likely to take steps to update their skills and knowledge.
>
> (*THES*, 17 May 2002)

He is quoting from a survey commissioned by the NIACE and completed in 2002.

Employers and employees

As soon as attention is switched from those groups in society to the other group that the government is so anxious about – employees – then encouraging wider participation in lifelong learning looks rather different. Not that the principles of successful encouragement differ; it is their application. For them, most of the obstacles which discourage the groups discussed so far are just as significant, the exception being that people in employment generally are not put off so much by formal institutions. Employment gives them a stake in the world. If they decide they need to learn more, then they will find it, and if that means a formal institution which they do not like, they can probably put up with it.

This is the case for what may be loosely categorised as two kinds of life-long learning: work-related and other. As the government never tires of repeating, there is an obvious need for work-related further learning. And there is the other, which can be characterised broadly as learning which is sought.

Employees in all types of employment and at all levels need to keep pace with the speed of technological changes and their impact, not merely on how work is done but the very nature of the work itself. Information technology develops at such a baffling speed that not enough people keep up with those changes. This is where skills shortages are bemoaned, but it is a mystery as to why some of these shortages persist. In part it is because for a long time recruitment to university degree courses in engineering skills has dwindled in some cases to the extent that departments have been closed for lack of students. The contribution of further education has not compensated for these reduced numbers. In turn this may have something to do with attitudes developed in schools. It means that there is an inadequate flow of new recruits to production industry. However, that does not explain why more employers are not more keen for more of their employees to develop their range of capabilities. It may be one of the consequences of relatively full employment. Even where there are large-scale redundancies, as in the car manufacturing business, it could be that many turn themselves into entrepreneurs of one kind or another and set up their own versions of small businesses so that they are not drawn back into mainstream industry. Perhaps it is lack of ambition to advance financially, socially, or perhaps it is just complacency on the part of both employers and employees. It is to be hoped that it is not lack of aptitude. Whatever it is, it is a serious failure of lifelong learning that for essentially economic reasons the skills shortage drum needs banging so loudly.

But people learn when they want to learn something, need to learn something. How then can more employees have their fancy tickled into positive motivation? This goes back to discouragements. Many of those discouragements can be removed by employers if they have a mind to do so. But that depends on employers generally subscribing to the notion that as well as tending their own profitability, it is part of their social responsibility to ensure that their own employees are kept up to date so that they continue to be employable as well as seeing that productivity is maximised. One of the perennial problems about getting employee development schemes established is that far and away the largest number of employees are in small and medium-sized companies. With narrow profit margins they cannot afford to send employees away on courses, and even if they could they cannot afford the loss of time for employees to be away from work. Most of the large employers need no prompting to promote the further training of their employees. Their productivity and profitability depends on it. So it is as it has been for many years; so what kinds of encouragement can be offered to small and medium-sized employers?

Motivation for adults

This is where the set of discouragements referred to above enters the picture. How can the motivation of employees be stimulated so that they engage in lifelong learning willingly? One incentive is to enable employees to do themselves some good at the same time that they are doing what an employer needs. Leaving wages to one side as outside the scope of this discourse the obvious way is to link whatever is learned to some credentialing system. Whether we like it or not we live in a credential age. Qualifications and the pieces of paper on which they are recorded matter hugely to increasing numbers of people. Employers do themselves some good by accepting that and working with it.

If that linkage with credentials can be associated with work-based learning as the primary vehicle for further learning, then employees may react more kindly to being told that they need to learn more. That means space again. If the prime object of getting more employees involved in lifelong learning is to enhance their performance at work through developing their skills and extending their knowledge, then there is everything to be gained by enabling them to do so at their place of work, unless there are compelling reasons against it. It is familiar; it is where they are; they do not have to travel to some other place for it. It is the same principle at work: take learning to where people are rather than expect them to go somewhere else for it.

There is more to it than that. If an employee really grasps that the employer's approach to work is that it is a place of learning as well as working, it can transform attitudes to further learning since it becomes not so much something being imposed but an invitation to learn more. Motivation can be stimulated at source.

Choice for adults

Perhaps even more important for encouragement is the range of choice offered to employees. So far references to lifelong learning for employees has been limited to training in the day-to-day activities of the business. But if the mental activity of learning is more important than the content of what is learned, then that applies to employees as well as anyone else. Productivity does not rest on skill and knowledge alone; attitudes affect it intimately. And there is no better way to encourage positive attitudes than by giving people a choice, in this case of what they are going to learn. Choosing means thinking, being alert. Alert individuals who are good at learning are what employers say they want. Alert individuals think, and their thinking is more important than what they think about because an alert individual can change the direction of the thinking.

This harks back to the proposition that too heavy a concentration on vocational and skills training can be self-defeating. Applied to employees it means that the route to strengthening people as thinking individuals may just as well be through studying literature, archaeology, ornithology, orienteering or gardening, food and cookery, as through polishing up engineering skills, learning the latest IT processes, or seminars on salesmanship. This is the learning which is sought, the second kind of employee learning. And if this appears fanciful, it is not.

Over a decade ago, Ford UK invented a programme for their employees called the Employee Development and Assistance Programme (EDAP). It was an adaptation of an extremely successful programme in the USA. Its purpose was to give a subsidised opportunity to each individual employee to engage in a learning programme of their own choice, provided it was not frivolous. The scheme was completely separate from Ford's in-house training for its employees. It was based on an agreement between the company and the trade unions that for every employee in each plant, a modest sum would be put into a fund to pay for EDAP.

Motivation was there from the start. Unions considered EDAP money as theirs. Moreover, EDAP funds could be used only for a learning programme that was not associated with the training programmes which Ford ran as a company to keep its workforce up to date with production methods and all that that entailed. This provision was guarded jealously by plant committees. Any application which looked as if it offended against this rule was rejected. Equally importantly, each plant ran its own EDAP programme. A joint committee of weekly paid, monthly paid and management serving in equal numbers elected its own chairman. It some cases a weekly paid production worker was chairman and in no case was someone from management in the chair. The committee controlled the programme for the plant. It considered applications for financial support for following a particular line of study and decided which to approve. It might be languages, bricklaying, history, house maintenance, even learning to drive.

Learning to drive illustrates the significance for the company of choice, attitude, and thus commitment to learning in an employee. For instance, a factory floor worker lived a long way from the nearest college of further education. Without a car and unable to drive, it was impossible for him to get to the college to take some language courses which he wanted to do. He applied for a grant to support him taking driving lessons. Equipped with a driving licence he submitted a further application for support to study French. This was with an eye on employment opportunities in Europe. A success story; it was a sophisticated version of access.

Trade unions

How far trade unions generally may have been influenced by EDAP is unclear, but the spirit of that programme informs the impressive development of the Union Learning Representative scheme which was introduced in the 1998 legislation. Within three years of its inception some 2000 ULRs had been recruited, trained and are now busy with their tasks.

Thus the ULR programme is an obvious vehicle for carrying further the lifelong learning message. One of the basic principles for seeking development in anything is to back winners. Their success then stands out as a beacon of achievement which can become a reference point for further development. The ULR programme is a case in point. Given its success and the evident enthusiasm for the scheme shown not only by the ULRs themselves but by those of their trade union colleagues who have been helped, encouraged and led into further learning, this is potentially a particularly fertile area of enterprise for the development of lifelong learning. If ever there was an initiative to encourage which could encourage others, this is one.

Voluntary organisations

Voluntary organisations are another obvious place to play the encouragement card. Their success in making large contributions to the development of lifelong learning over the years indicates that if the government is serious about it in the long term then enabling these organisations to deploy their expertise more widely is bound to be a good use of scarce resources.

Civic sense and democracy

The people who made the decisions in the EDAP programme to first fund a worker to take driving lessons and then to take courses in French were his peers. In each of the plants male and female representatives of the three groups which made up EDAP committees – hourly paid, weekly paid and management – were having to make decisions about which applications from fellow workers to approve or reject, leading to difficult and sometimes controversial decisions and living with the results. This was serious. As the news about the facilities offered by EDAP spread, committees were inundated with applications, not all of which could be funded with the budget. To a certain extent their horizons were widened. Industrial democracy mingled with what were essentially civic responsibilities.

This leads to another highly significant aspect of EDAP. In the USA the scheme was introduced at the time when large numbers of employees were losing their jobs and further reductions in staffing levels were assumed to be coming in the future. An essential purpose of the programme there was to help those workers become more employable through studying in areas where they assumed that employment prospects might be good. In many cases men and women studied courses which led to a formal qualification. Whatever they studied it was in the interests of the company as a means of trying to ensure that as many as possible of those put out of work remained economically productive members of society. However, this was not the basic reason for the company financing the scheme, which was extended to spouses. Its eye was on labour relations. The more humanely it handled such large-scale 'let goes' as the Americans say, the fewer problems there would be in the future.

In this country, whatever Ford's motives, something of the same applied, namely to do what it could to help its workers find alternative employment if they needed it. Participation rates shot up. No one complained that workers were being less productive at work; rather the reverse. Managers made connections between EDAP users and levels of morale, none of which is surprising. Give individuals a choice about what they want to learn, and support their efforts, and they are likely to be people who are more pleased with themselves and the world. Civic implications again. And it is bottom-up development.

The ULR representatives are in the same category. They are volunteers drawn from their own union who may or may not be shop stewards, but they are making efforts to convince fellow union members of the value of learning among their peers. It is bottom-up again.

The voluntaries make a similar point. No one joins in any learning programme there if they do not wish to. They live by the bottom-up principle.

Lifelong learning in the round

This is where the learning which is sought and chosen connects with the learning which is necessary for economic reasons. The first can feed the second. Take away the compulsory element or anything which smacks of it from the second and, prompted by the first, there is a greater likelihood that people will be more willing to engage with the second. This is like one of the tricks of seeing at night with the naked eye. Look just a little off to the side of the object and the object will be seen more clearly. Developing the capacities which employers value is rather like that. Do not aim too precisely at the desired outcome. Aim off centre and the target may be met.

It is easy to cite the Ford EDAP programme as if it is the solution to all updating problems. That cannot be, given that the majority of people are employed in small and medium-sized businesses. But the principles on which EDAP is based can be put to work. In the early 1990s what was then the Kent Training and Enterprise Council developed its own version of an EDAP for small companies. It drew on a report on EDAP conducted for the Department of Employment by the Learning from Experience Trust. By devising arrangements whereby the TEC would use some of its publicly provided funds as individual bursaries for individuals to attend courses of their own choosing which were then negotiated with local colleges, it shared with employers the cost of loss of time and productivity that the company forfeited through the individual not being on the company's premises. It also took away from the employer the burden of dealing with education bodies on behalf of the employees. It was lifelong learning at a practical level.

In other words, with some imagination employee development pro-grammes can be devised for companies of all sizes. However, doing so does depend on officials showing some ingenuity in interpreting rules and financial requirements and being prepared to take risks. This refers back to questions of trust and of decentralisation.

Democracy

Through schemes such as Ford's EDAP and other employee development schemes where choice is available to employees, lifelong learning takes on an utterly different significance. It relates to participant democracy. It is the third essential context for encouragement. It is no good politicians complaining that fewer and fewer people bother to vote in elections if they do not try some joined-up thinking in parallel with supposed benefits of joined-up government.

Voting can be either a knee-jerk performance, a deliberate act of support for a political party or a thoughtful response to a range of uncer-tainties. The decline in voting is a reflection of the fewer number of people who are automatically supportive of political parties. A better educated population living in a world of uncertainties ensures that. So far it looks as if that decline in those numbers has not been replaced by growing numbers of thoughtful, uncertain voters. To increase those numbers means reducing the levels of cynicism which politicians have brought on themselves, and to do that requires engaging people in thinking.

This is where the two previous contextual factors for encouragement come together. If government loosens central controls, gets out of the way of professionals who are wanting to promote lifelong learning, stops being so obsessive about vocational training, and reforms its mode of funding, then there is a chance that through up-to-date versions of liberal educa-tion more people will be thinking more about things which matter to them and to the country in its global position. It may incline them to think more about social matters. If that could be the case, then lifelong learning would be doing its most important job.

That would merely be setting a more suitable scene for action than exists at present. To make a real difference in the country a means has to be found of harnessing together in some collaborative way all the efforts which are put into lifelong learning variously through LEAs. LSCs, trade unions, voluntary and community bodies, NIACE, VSNTO, open learning networks, further and higher education, and the government itself. That is the route to encouraging wider participation.

However, there is one essential proviso to any such plans for collaborative signposting encouragement for wider participation: terms of staff employment. There is little point in talking about flexible arrangements to benefit adult learners if there is not a matching set of flexible arrangements for employing those who are expected to provide the service for those adults. This is explored in Chapter 7.

Chapter 7

Widening participation – doing it

Government leading from the front

Doing it means doing something different. It means government leading from the front because what has been done so far does not work well enough; there needs to be a review of policy. Thus doing it differently means the government paying attention to a list of things which it alone can do. It means getting rid of its obsessions with micro-management and the vocational version of lifelong learning. It means the Treasury dropping its obsession with bean counting as a means of policing the use of public funds. It means also the Treasury adopting accounting systems which are flexible, designed deliberately to accommodate risks of failure so as to free up the LSC and formal institutions to get on with their job. It means exploiting the experience and expertise of voluntary bodies and trade unions. Of fundamental importance if the drive for lifelong learning is a serious element in public policy is to reconsider how secondary schools can become a better preparation for lifelong learning. Above all it means the government replacing rhetoric with leading from the front through coherent action promoted by joined-up government to bring the Department for Education and Skills, the Department for Work and Pensions, the Treasury and the Cabinet Office into line.

But doing it also needs something else. Flexible arrangements for space, place, content, pedagogy for adult learners, need flexible staffing arrangements to support them.

Staffing

As in every walk of life so it is with education; everything depends on people, their attitudes and demeanour, their self-perception of their role and the way they are regarded by others and the extent to which they feel valued. No matter what attempts are made to move significantly towards widening participation, all will come to nought unless there are radical rearrangements in the conditions of service for men and women who work in this field as well as in the institutions themselves. It is no good pleading for flexibility in curriculum, place and time where it is offered, tacitly asking those institutions to transform themselves unless there is comparable flexibility in the way the work is staffed.

One of the key reasons for the success of university extramural and WEA branches was that all such institutional questions were in the hands of members. It was the group or WEA branch which decided not only what they wanted to learn but when, where and at what time. Tutors who taught these classes either accepted those conditions or refused them and risked having no classes to teach. True, most tutors were not on the permanent staff, working as part-timers, but the full-time staff worked to just those requirements. Similarly, if serious attempts are made to engage some of the 'missing', let alone expand the overall participation rate in some form of lifelong learning, the same principles need to become the norm for those who are going to help them learn.

Without taking the devolution argument to its logical conclusion where each institution made up its own rules for pay and conditions, there ought to be some way of loosening the terms of national agreements which at their worst seem to block any move towards flexibility as unions and employers fight their respective corners. Suppose individuals had a choice about the terms under which they prefer to be employed. There could be two forms of contracts for full-time staff. One would be a continuation of present further education regulations, with detailed specifications of hours and so on. No threat then to current conditions which had been won the hard negotiating way. The other could be an open-ended commitment where in effect staff would serve at the pleasure of the Principal, creating a group of licensed outriders for lifelong learning development. No one would be required to enter into such an open-ended commitment; it would be volunteers only. By agreement they would be able to respond to the circumstances peculiar to a particular group at whatever time was appropriate and for however long it took. The institution would become far more responsive than is usually the case.

Perhaps the second contract would need to include benefits for accepting its open-endedness; a kind of bonus for being an entrepreneurial operator who did not count hours. It would resemble the youth tutors who were appointed in some schools following the Newsom Report. If entrepreneurial activity is sought then entrepreneurs have to be set free. Without that there is no enterprise.

If this form of flexibility of employment were available, it could be that in parallel the balance between full-time and part-time staff should be changed. As a succession of jobs over a lifetime becomes the norm for more people, the personal portfolio of employment idea, with people mixing full-time and part-time work and no work according to the way they want to live, an increase in part-time work for lifelong learning would seem to fit the bill. Apart from anything else it is almost impossible for the full-time staff of an institution to respond to the unpredictable curricula demands which follow on from the kind of institution flexibility being discussed. A great deal of FE work is already undertaken by part-time staff and always has been. But in the search for ways of making institutions more able to respond to demands which cannot be known in advance, perhaps there ought to be more of them and fewer full-timers. This frees up an institution to find someone who can tutor a group in, say, underwater exploration and another for urban traffic control when the full-time staff are not so competent to do so.

This is where the second form of contract could be valuable. Full-time staff serving at the pleasure of the Principal could be dispatched to seek out new possibilities for developing further learning activities, and part-time staff could be found to do the teaching. However, because part-timers by definition do not have the same sense of personal security as do full-time staff, whatever their legal position, paying part-timers an entrepreneurial bonus for that form of personal risk might be an important inducement. Just as full-timers who are on an open-ended contract would be paid in effect for working unsocial hours, perhaps in strange places with strange people, so part-timers could be paid for accepting a different form of risk. This would lift the status of part-timers by abandoning the current hourly rate which always seems somehow demeaning. At the very least, part-time staff should be paid pro rata of their full-time colleagues. It could be a way of getting high-quality service and value for money, and the institution could benefit. If such a demand for underwater exploration or urban traffic control could not be met, the institution loses some of its recruitment numbers. If it could find staff to meet those curricula demands, then its recruitment numbers would go up and the annual budget would look more healthy.

Discussing these issues in relation to lifelong learning is of course only one example of a general issue. Whether for public or private company employees in this modern technological age, changes in ways of living have not been mirrored in ways of working. It is another massive mismatch and is not unconnected with notions of citizenship.

Of course it is risky. There are huge disadvantages in employing large number of part-time staff, but they have to be set against the disadvantages of having too few. It is a question of balancing two categories of risk. One of the main thrusts of this book is to say that without taking risks there is no possibility of making significant headway with turning numbers of the 'missing' into participants. If it is right, however unlikely, for the government to be persuaded to take risks deliberately to facilitate developments and experiments, then the same has be true for providers. Institutions and their staff need to be set free to do whatever makes sense in their locality. But if educational institutions are to grow up and take their proper place in the fast-changing world in which people live, they have to change. Almost everything else in sight has changed, become flexible, uncertain, as a way of living. If that is the way adults now live their lives, then institutions have to follow suit unless they want to find themselves superseded by private entrepreneurs on the internet. The beginning to the twenty-first century is crying out for adult institutions, but they cannot become such without changing their ways. That means rethinking how to make the best use of the staff available.

Micro-management/mismanagement

Even under the most favourable conditions for staff, at present any thoughts about how to do things in ways which are different from all the attempts so far run into the same obstruction: micro-management by government. Schools, further and higher education and voluntary bodies are all held like fish behind a dam and released into a complicated set of fine-meshed nets designed to keep out everything which does not fit the predetermined size of what has official approval. For as long as regulations operate in this way, there is little likelihood of lifelong learning going anywhere interesting, or doing it differently. Going to interesting places will have to wait until those regulations are changed and central administration foregoes its attempts to police every move and instead reverts to its proper job, namely creating the conditions under which professionals can do their job through moving to a strategic position. That is what administration is for.

The point is well made by three distinguished professors, who have issued what amount to proclamations about how not to do it. One is John Field who has a solid track record of developing lifelong learning as well as being an adviser to the Labour government. Another is Tim Brighouse, who moved in and out of local government administration and higher education and ended up as Chief Education Officer for the City of Birmingham. He too is an adviser to the Labour government and for a period was Co-chairman of the Secretary of State's Standards' Committee. The third is Alan Smithers, Sydney Jones Professor of Education and Director of the Centre for Education and Employment Research at the University of Liverpool. We know that the government tends to be suspicious of professors but since two of these have advised government itself and the third has undertaken serious research on behalf of the government, it is reasonable to suppose that they might be listened to.

Field helped to draft the government's blueprint on lifelong learning in 1997. However, in an address of the Universities Association of Continuing Education he warned that the government's lifelong learning policy was set to run into the buffers, as almost every initiative has flopped (*THES*, 5 April 2002). He spoke of 'initiative-itis' as a way of describing the almost relentless flow of requirements which emerge from the DfES. He said: 'it is hard to see a single one which has been a success story.' He listed the non-success stories such as individual lifelong learners vouchers. Then, like many others, he pointed to the embarrassment caused by the target set to reach 50 per cent of the under-thirties' participating in higher education by 2010. The reclassification of non-award-bearing courses, especially of short courses where mature students do not sit examinations, skews the figures. As was predicted at the time, he reminded his audience that it would be a rerun of the Diploma of Higher Education in the late 1970s if Blunkett's much-trumpeted Foundation Degree scheme failed to engage the 18 to 30-year-olds and so did not fulfil its intended purpose. The misnamed University of Industry has not lived up to expectations. The imaginative introduction of the scheme for individual learning accounts was closed as a result of financial fraud. It could even be said that this last failure is the most serious because of its potential to support wider participation. He seems to imply a busted flush. And talking to a university audience, Field said, 'However, lifelong learning will not go away and universities will have to invent their own futures in a context where lifelong learning poses unavoidable challenges.'

As far as higher education goes this seems like a rehearsal of the ways of not widening participation. But Field did go on to complain that too little attention was paid to research in further education because he asserted that there was no intellectual rationale for it. Since it is from this level that most of the wider participation in lifelong learning is assumed to come, that is a very serious criticism. Perhaps this is one of the challenges for higher education that he refers to. It certainly relates to access policies in higher education and asks questions about the status of qualifications and their relation to what has now become gold standard controversies for AS and A level examinations.

Transposed on to the national map for lifelong learning, this points to the clash between schemes due to run into the buffers and 'unavoidable challenges'. The unhappy aspect to this is that it is not for want of trying that the government finds itself in this predicament. The 'initiative-itis' that Field refers to is indicative of the government's serious intentions. How can it be then that the investment of time in consultations, papers and publications, ministerial exhortation and, to some extent, money, has so little to show for it?

It is also noteworthy that Professor David Robinson of Liverpool John Moore's University, who advised the government on both learning accounts and the Foundation Degree, referred in a lecture to the Social Market Foundation to what he claimed were necessary reforms to make a success of it (*THES*, 24 May 2002). Saying the unthinkable, he speculated that cheaper fees for the Foundation degree than for an honours degree might lead to larger enrolments. In effect this would create a further two-tiered division. And, like Field, he reckoned that further education ought to be leading the initiative rather than universities.

Tim Brighouse did not concentrate on lifelong learning but his approach to the question 'How many are to be successful?' in the paper he gave at a lecture at the Royal Society of Arts in April 2002 offered different perspectives on the topic. In the course of his address he pointed to two areas where he thought the government has gone seriously wrong. While welcoming the dilution of some of the oppressive dictats of the National Curriculum, he claimed that an over-concentration on the three Rs plus IT was a disservice to children in primary schools. Instead, he said:

> Schools need to be encouraged to rethink their use of time so that children whose different talents are developing at different speeds have experiences which will boost their confidence and give them a taste of success rather than seeing themselves labelled as comparative failures in the three Rs. That is not to argue against the emphasis on those vital basic skills, but it is to underline that if you have experienced comparative failure in those skills, and that has been seen by the school, your parents and society as the sole measure of success, you are liable to switch off education and fail to find the talent and confidence from which you can succeed.

He carried that through, recognising individual differences to secondary education with the one-liner: 'secondary education is not the same as secondary schools.' He quoted the oft-used piece on adolescence from *The Winter's Tale*:

> I would there were no age between sixteen and three and twenty, or that youth would sleep out the rest; for there is nothing in between but getting wenches with child, wronging the ancientry, stealing, fighting...

This was to make the point that all this is even more pertinent these days as, for many, peer group influence has largely taken over from parental influence. After claiming that none of the attempts to improve the service through all the versions of magnet schools would work, his suggestion for providing a better service for all adolescents is to group secondary schools into collegiate groups which between them will offer learning opportunities across the entire curriculum. His accent was on all pupils, not merely some.

Taking primary and secondary schooling in this way he made it clear that in his view the present arrangements were a poor foundation on which to build hopes for wider participation in lifelong learning. He went on to criticise the government's heavy, never-ending centralising policy as being more Stalinist than Stalinists with its concentration on management, auditing and bureaucracy.

Indeed one of the ironies is that at the same time that the Berlin Wall came down and the East was encouraged to copy our Western Ways, we moved in exactly the opposite direction. Some of the centralist measures would not discredit the church states of the 17th century.

(Brighouse 2002)

Put together, those two passages may be construed as a critique of a too great emphasis on instrumental and vocational education and a frontal attack on over-centralisation. Brighouse made it clear that both were related to what he called the demeaning treatment of teachers by central governments over the past fifteen years: 'Their treatment is based on complete mistrust.' And there we have it. Trust.

An implication of Field's objection to initiative-itis is that the government does not trust practitioners to get on with the job of developing life-long learning without precise briefs to follow. Lack of trust no less. Brighouse's explicit accusation of the government's demeaning of teachers amounting to a withdrawal of trust sings the same song.

Alan Smithers takes up the criticism of the government's Stalinist-style policies. Commenting on the boost to funds for education in the 2002 Chancellor's Economic Review he said:

[I]t [the review] illustrates vividly how much current thinking about education is being distorted by Government's attempts to manage centrally the education system through targets in the manner of a defunct socialist republic.

Quite why ministers should have gone down this road in education and in health is not clear. After all they [ministers] ruled out a social-ist economy. But the outcomes could have been easily foreseen from what happened in Eastern Europe.

If rewards and sanctions are attached to attaining targets, managers will focus on them at the expense of other, more important, goals. Everything possible will be done to reach the specified numbers, but if they are unattainable there will be a tendency to make them up.

That is the case for administration. Equally serious are the unfortunate consequences on the education of pupils. Smithers says of tests and targets in primary schools:

Not surprisingly, hot housed primary pupils pause for breath in the early secondary years. This dip has recently led to great concern on the part of government and the inspectorate. Their response; more targets. Almost the first pronouncement from the new Chief Inspector was to propose targets for 12 year olds. There are however already targets for 14 year olds which are being pursued through a Key Stage 3 strategy costing £200 million a year.

(*Independent*, 11 July 2002)

Had he been writing a couple of months later he could have cited the shambles of the A and AS level results as incontrovertible evidence of the baleful consequences of trying to control 'standards' bureaucratically.

These indictments are not from airy-fairy researchers of the kind so disliked by government. They are sober, considered judgements by men with impressive records of service with practical achievements based on working closely in the day-to-day practice of education. Is it possible that in agreement they are so far off the nub of the matter? The wonder is that the government seems deaf to them, especially as it is serious about widening participation. Perhaps it confuses itself by its much complained-about tendency to select and manipulate research findings.

All this means that there is a danger that lifelong learning may be seen as yet another example of an unrealised wish list: laudable intentions being wished on the country without the resources to turn policy into action. Education on the cheap yet again. While this is true it is not the whole story, the more significant part of which lies in the explorations in Chapter 6 about finding ways towards widening participation. The deduction from this is that the government is simply approaching the issue in the wrong way. In its laudable anxiety to get things done it issues a stream of new initiatives – initiative-itis – which become directives, few of which are absorbed properly before the next set comes through the post; short-term solutions for long-term problems. The answer has to be that it needs to reverse its instinctive centralising tendency. It has to accept that there are many people who are more capable of achieving wider participation than anyone in government or the Civil Service, and that the sooner it gets out of their way the better. It has to begin to trust people to do the job and stop looking over their shoulders all the time.

During the controversy in the 1970s about teacher training and the role of school-based training – it continues – there was a simple way of resolving the relationship between schools and training institutions. It was to ask the direct question: What is it that schools can do and colleges cannot and what is it that colleges can do that schools cannot? Answer that and the roles become clear. It is the same with government and lifelong learning. It needs to ask what it can and ought to do which no one else can, and what it is that it cannot do but others can.

The really difficult thing for the government in trying to answer this question is that it alone can move out of the way. If real progress is to be made in the range and volume of participation in lifelong learning then the government has to steel itself for a self-denying ordinance and loosen the lines of executive control in a whole range of directions and restore some status to professionals. It alone can set the scene for more effective approaches to lifelong learning. This is where the doing has to begin.

However, the increase in funding for public services including education announced by the Chancellor in July 2002 makes it all the more difficult for the government to stop trying to manage everything from the centre, for beginning the doing where it counts most. In its anxiety and need to convince the public that as a result of spending more money to improve services it invented even more stringent and numerous policing devices. No doubt horrid memories of some of the antics of local government turn to nightmares of things going wrong. Centralisation is designed to prevent that. But it is as if for the most laudable of reasons the government has increased funds for public services as an act of faith in itself as being able to implement the reforms without which services will not improve, while at the same time demonstrating in a very public way that it has very limited faith in the ability of the people who work in the services to achieve those improvements without being bullied. Of course the government should worry about waste and ill-judged financial expenditure, but excessive supervision will not ensure that this does not happen. All the evidence of the years of the Labour government from 1997 onward confirms that view. Thus once again the government is simultaneously providing the means to do the job while making it less likely that the job will be done fully. Audit trails need interrogating.

Perhaps it is hubris stemming from the relatively successful management of the economy so far that makes government believe in its own capacity to micro-manage from the centre, when manifestly it is incompetent to do so. Perhaps it reflects a collective sense of insecurity and fear of the consequences of delegation and devolution. The mystery is why this lesson has not yet been learned. It bodes ill for lifelong learning.

Hence the starting point for trying to find answers to the question of how to do it – increase participation – lies there. Less micro-management from the centre, fewer attempts to measure performance by detailed surveillance. In a word more trust, more autonomy, more devolution.

Schooling

Let us take schooling first. Primary schooling is in general up to scratch, or coming up. Secondary schooling is a different matter. Brighouse's distinction between secondary education and secondary schools is vital. Systems may seem fine. Publicly published score cards may appear to confirm their effectiveness. What they do not show is how far those students who do not score well are having an appropriate form of education. Hence his title for that lecture: 'How many are to be successful?'

If secondary schools are to be serious about preparing their pupils to be lifelong learners there are difficult curriculum questions to be faced. Those questions have to try to find answers which would persuade those students who are among the potential 'missing' to becoming lifelong learner participants in the future. They are those who drop out of AS/A level courses. They are those who feel failures at age 16 and so fade away as learners. And there are the truants and poor school attenders who act so as to outdisplay their disenchantment. They need time, space and place, just as do older adults.

For about forty-five years discussion has run on and on about broadening the sixth-form curriculum. In its heyday the Schools' Council produced a series of comprehensive reports. Ministers dither, uncertain what to do, fearing an onslaught on whatever they do from the Gold Standard brigade, even if they are not members of it themselves. Now the ill-thought-out AS levels, as their originator, the current headmaster of Winchester College, admits, have added intolerable burdens to both students for whom it was supposed to offer opportunities for studying more broadly, and to their staff who have to prepare students for yet another examination, both being held in hock by league tables. Watching and hearing of the pressures being experienced by their peers, reluctant learners are hardly likely to be encouraged to become energetic learners. Those experiences are precisely what they do not want.

Simultaneously, and this time more urgently, debate is beginning to run about scrapping GCSE. The claim is that it serves no useful purpose now that policy is designed to keep as many young men and women in full-time education beyond the age of 16. As a school-leaving certificate it has served its time. With AS level piled on top, it is turning schools into cramming institutions with little time for students to learn anything, let alone enjoy it. Once again the international baccalaureate is entering the argument.

Using GCSE results as a bench-mark for defining success or failure also forces schools to follow a curriculum for all pupils which everyone knows is unsuitable for a number of 15/16-year-olds in almost any school. It drives teachers to teach for tests and pupils to remember what examiners want. This is bad enough for the bright students who can sail smoothly through examinations, but it does little to encourage adventurousness in learning. For a large number of others it is wholly inappropriate. It is the twenty-first-century version of the nineteenth-century gradgrind, and as a launching pad for subsequent lifelong learning it is disastrous. It is far too narrow and bureaucratically organised. Abandoning it would free up schools to design their own range of curricula for their own range of pupils as learning experiences and as a launching pad for A levels for the majority who continued to want to take them as their main course, with a fair assumption that they would see the point of lifelong learning later on.

With GCSE gone as a hurdle for 16-year-olds, and the loosening of the

National Curriculum at the other end, schools could set about devising curricula which had all their students' needs as a reference point: a devolved curriculum. Academic subjects and study would remain. For those for whom that was not the best way of learning, programmes would centre on aspects of themselves, their town or area, the country and the world which interested them. Skilful teachers are well able to integrate essential elements of the formal curriculum with such an approach. Add properly organised periods of work experience in public and private undertakings, assignments in voluntary and community organisations where the object was to learn and not just be there for the experience of it. With such a curriculum it would be highly likely that some of the alleged non-academic students would find their way back into academic study. If they learned what interested them, motivation might strengthen them for more learning. Such a group could stay together with the same teacher for much of the week in a settled base. A sense of being special could develop. Some coherence to school life could replace the essential fragmentation of contemporary timetables.

A school-designed set of learning programmes could act as an aperitif for something more substantial. Suppose some fifteen young men and women did not want to follow AS and A level syllabuses, but needed a good reason for staying on beyond age 16. A talented teacher with those kinds of students could turn them into a learning group. As well as paying attention to the types of literacy, numeracy and IT skills they would need to secure employment, much of the curriculum could be in response to what the members of the group would like to learn about. Nothing would be off limits with the teacher's tasks being those of a learning leader as a generalist who knows how to gain access to the necessary materials without being an expert, and who can spot the opportunities for engaging in what in technical terms are known as social skills. Add in some work experience which is designed especially as a mode of learning, and a range of visits to places which members of the group say they are interested in visiting. Allocate a space which the group could make their own. Ignore conventional timetable and attendance formal requirements. Let the headteacher get on with it, intervening only when disaster threatened.

No doubt such a scheme will be dismissed as hopelessly idealistic or the dreaded word progressive. As seen at present no doubt it is. The sad, indeed distressing, fact is that the Humanities Curriculum Project led by Lawrence Stenhouse in the late 1960s and early 1970s demonstrated successfully that such schemes or modifications of them were very effective ways of engaging young people in serious issues which concerned them. Compulsory lessons in citizenship, the latest initiative-itis thrust on schools, could offer a contemporary opportunity to do something similar. The Speaker's Commission on Citizenship based its thinking on T.H. Marshall's book *Citizenship and Social Class* (Marshall 1991). His view of

citizenship was fourfold: civil liberty, freedom of speech, political participation in the exercise of power and social economic security. In the
THES Millennium issue Fay Weldon wrote: 'we are educated not to
become wise and help build a good society, but so that we can get good
jobs and spend our earnings.' Given a lighter National Curriculum
requirement, many teachers are perfectly capable of inspiring adolescents
in exploring some of those issues. They just need time and space to do so.
It could be civic renewal. And they do not need to be told how to do it.

Explorations of that kind become ethical. In a relatively godless society,
many parents and their offspring are all at sea with automatic understandings of what is right and wrong. Some things are applauded (celebrity-
itis), and others punished (getting caught). There is what seems to be
acceptable and what is not acceptable behaviour and that is the end of it.
This is the stuff of citizenship. With some imagination it could bring the
curriculum to life.

Any attempt to develop secondary schools as effective launching pads
for further learning needs to think along these lines, especially when the
potentially 'missing' are included in the plans. It is no more than accepting that these young people are in fact young adults and that it is only
common sense to treat them as such. Like adults they need to be able to
choose. How else can learning be used to help develop any sense of personal responsibility?

But then there is the question of premises: where should all this take
place? In parallel with arguments about the sixth-form curriculum similar
arguments have raged about whether post-16 education should be in
sixth-form or further education colleges. Understandably, heads want to
retain all the academic and financial benefits which go with sixth-form
study as well as the invaluable social and community benefits from having
young men and women in a school community. Alternatively, many argue
that the adult atmosphere of a further education college or sixth-form
college is far more suitable for growing adolescents. There will never be
an either-or answer. What does make sense is for students to be able to
choose where they would prefer to be for post-16 study. Given the uneven-
ness of both school and further education provision the obvious answer is
for both to be grouped in some sort of cluster so that each school or
college could concentrate on its strengths: what Brighouse called collegiate groupings.

Freed to act, imaginations could get to work. Apart from the necessary
insurance and health and safety matters, there is no particular reason why
such 16-plus provision should be in either school or college. A place
where growing young men and women can meet as learners while feeling
relaxed and unthreatened is just as important for them as it is for some
of the missing adult participants considered above. Looked at in this
way there would be some chance of establishing secondary and post-16

learning, as an intentional way of creating a launching pad for lifelong learning for succeeding generations.

However, there is an intrinsic difficulty about approaching any such development in government plans for reforming secondary education. Increasing specialisation between differing secondary schools may or may not be an improvement. What is clear is that there will be no common denominator to their development and no common status. The risk is that it will be another version of close concentration on institutional reorganisation and utterly inadequate attention being paid to what the reformed institutions are to do educationally for their pupils. It is no good just sticking new labels, titles and addresses on newly reformed secondary schools. What matters is what kind of learning its teachers are able to encourage.

General Teachers Council

Once upon a time there was the Schools Council, which acted as a central research body to explore precisely these curricula issues among the many other things it did. It drew on the experience and expertise of schoolteachers and heads, lecturers in further and higher education, unions and professional associations, local authority advisers with HMIs who both advised and acted as government watch-dogs. It disappeared amidst the rubble of Tory education demolition. Now there is the General Teachers Council which is trying to find its feet. Perhaps it is time to expand its brief and role to include curriculum development. It could convene groups to review the curriculum independently of government. This could serve the government more reliably than the ad hoc collection of education whiz-kids who populate think-tanks and act as official advisers. If its eye was focused sharply on preparation for lifelong learning, schools might become attractive to the many young people who currently find them irrelevant.

Post-compulsory secondary education

When 'doing it differently' is related to higher education the picture is quite different. Insofar as widening participation at undergraduate level is concerned it may be seen as a preparation for wider participation in lifelong learning later on, and there is not a great deal more that universities can do unless they develop an additional range of outreach activities. Long before ministers became excited about numbers of admissions from the lower economic groups and from state schools, many a university was dismayed that despite their best efforts to find them, proportionately those numbers had not increased over the past twenty-five years. And it was not for want of trying to recruit them. Summer taster courses, open days, school visits, they were all there in some form or other. If greater efforts are to be made to change the pattern of admissions it has to be staffed properly.

The government is showing signs of accepting this through special funding arrangements. Castigating universities for not doing more when they have barely enough funding to serve their students in attendance is hardly calculated to persuade them to change. Doing more has to be paid for and the government has to face up to that fact.

Beyond that form of participation as a contribution to the development of lifelong learning some universities have substantial outreach activities and have had for many years. The prospectus of any of the former poly-technics shows a substantial provision at sub-degree level, aimed deliber-ately at recruiting men and women from the lower economic groups. Goldsmiths College of the University of London has its Department of Professional and Continuing Education which recruits annually over 2,000 students, many of whom are drawn from the ethnic groups in the heavily urban area of South-east London. Or there is the College of London created in the London Metropolitan University with a specifically explicit brief to devise new versions of outreach.

What prevents universities from doing more is to a large extent the result of funding mechanisms. The complications of obtaining funds to support these activities whether from the HEFCE or from the newly estab-lished LSCs do not make for easy development. Some, seeking to promote these very activities, apply to the European Commission, but there are limits to the amount of sub-degree work which some universities should undertake. Much depends on where they are in relation to their own immediate area.

Funding is also an obstacle for further education colleges developing imaginative schemes for LLL. There are two key issues: pay and policing. There is something bizarre about a situation where someone leaving, say, with an HND in engineering can begin work with a larger salary than the lecturers who taught him. Under these conditions recruiting high-quality staff, never mind retaining them, is a formidable obstacle to improving the performance of many a college. The same kind of thinking needs to inform pay and conditions of employment for further and for that matter higher education staff as has been deployed for reconsidering pay and conditions of school staff.

Furthermore, as long as funding is tied tightly to numbers of qualifica-tions awarded, their scope for manoeuvre is very limited. Even though the LSC has announced that non-vocational programmes will be treated on the same financial basis as courses leading to vocational qualifications, it is an open question how far that will release colleges to pursue their own devices in expanding their lifelong learning provision. Moreover, the tendency to perpetuate those distinctions is bound to make it that much more difficult to promote lifelong learning successfully.

Thus for post-secondary developments in lifelong learning it all depends on money. And that leads directly back to over-centralisation and attempted micro-management by government.

The Treasury

It would be the tail trying to wag the dog to say that lifelong learning is one among many public activities which would benefit if the Chancellor and the Treasury stopped behaving like an overlord for all departments. This is a political and constitutional issue which will either be resolved when powerful cabinet ministers insist on running their own shows or some bold soul separates the two functions. This is the trust issue at Cabinet level.

If this is not practical then there is something that the Treasury can and should do which is eminently practicable, and which touches deeply on the centralising tendency. This is about accounting systems and the use of public funds, and it is about shifting its weight from a solid risk-averse stance to a limited acceptance of risk. The society in which lifelong learning will flourish is a risk society.

Almost any enterprise, whether public or private, finds it almost impossible to meet precisely whatever performance criteria may be laid down. Circumstances change; key personnel come and go. The economy goes up and down, taking employment and unemployment with it. In these circumstances the bean-counting approach to the scrutiny of the use of public funds is therefore flawed and likely to fail. League tables, waiting lists, regulators' targets when imposed from above may be useful for politicians but they can produce extremely misleading information. Nowhere is this more true than in education and within education, and therefore for lifelong learning. Target setting from above cannot result in what is hoped to be achieved. Target setting from below is quite a different matter.

By definition the development of lifelong learning is an entrepreneurial activity. By implication the role of central government is to promote it. Often one of the most important results from special projects undertaken by a voluntary body, or some new line of development taken by a local authority or a LSC within its block grant, is something which no one dreamed would happen. It was not part of the design. It was not in the contract. It was not funded officially. But it can become a beacon for future activity. Somewhere along the line things took a turn which no one expected, and in strict terms might even be in violation of the contract for the work. That does not make it any less important. Thus Treasury regulations need adjusting to make it easier for those civil servants who have oversight of their own area of public service to use their own initiative instead of infuriating practitioners with what appears to be mindless obstruction but which is only the civil servants faithfully carrying out their brief. It seems ridiculous that able men and women are so fearful of contravening regulations that they have so little power to use their own judgement when unintended, unexpected success stares them in the face. This in no way diminishes the need for there to be a proper and rigorous accountability of the use of public funds. It is simply a way of injecting some common sense into a necessary activity. It is Onora O'Neill's point.

It may seem far-fetched but this could be the most potent act which the government can take to promote lifelong learning. Its effect would reach down through the LSC, local authorities and voluntary bodies. Simultaneously it would free up entrepreneurially minded practitioners to try things out which offered new approaches and were designed for a particular set of circumstances. It would also enable middle-ranking civil servants to back bright ideas when they were proposed to them. It would reinstate trust as an operating principle. Not so long ago this was the case.

Towards the end of the 1980s under the Tories' tax-cutting regime the Treasury put pressure on the Manpower Services Commission to justify its spending. This heralded the introduction of open bidding for contracts under project headings devised by officials within the Department of Employment. From that time on the manoeuvring room for officials to back bright ideas has been progressively reduced. It was a way of appearing to avoid taking risks with public funds at the same time as creating accountability systems which checked their proper use. The catalogue of failures which Professor Field referred to hardly suggests that open bidding with strict performance criteria is a convincing success.

As a result it became increasingly difficult for bright ideas to find a home. And so for education development stagnated in some ways, being limited to what was considered by government to be priorities and controlled by the centre.

The Learning and Skills Council

The argument so far about how to achieve wider participation involving those who do not participate at present is that essentially it depends on two lines of action which only the government can take if it is to fulfil its proper role. In both cases it simply has to get out of the way. The first is revising accountancy and accountability requirements for the use of public funds. The second is to stop obsessing about vocational education as the salvation of the economy. Both would be steps back from trying to micro-manage activities. Both are the essential prerequisites for creating the conditions under which lifelong learning can get on with expanding itself. Doing both would mean that the government had accepted that, if people are encouraged to do what they want to do instead of what government would like them to do, policies and funding have a good chance of achieving what they set out to achieve. The scene would be set for Brighouse's Stalinism to give way to Perestroika, and for Field's disease of central initiative-itis to be replaced by healthy responses to local needs and wishes.

These changes have a fundamental national significance because the LSC is now at one stage removed down from central government. As such, it has to act according to the conditions laid down by the government. Huge responsibilities and funds have been invested in this new body, but it will fail if it has to act as a kind of repeating machine for current systems of control, accountability and transparency imposed by the Treasury. Even if the LSC manages to act consistently on the commitment given by its chief executive at its beginning, that henceforth there will be a level playing field for the funding of activities by both public institutions and voluntary bodies, and that non-vocational courses are to be treated on the same basis financially as vocational courses, if the two prerequisites for expansion are not met – namely reform of the public accountability systems and the ending of attempts to control the curriculum for economic purposes – it will fail as all its predecessors have failed.

If the LSC had a licence to act in the spirit of the flexibility which would follow, then the possibilities for expanding lifelong learning will be transformed. It would enable it in part to focus sharply on efforts to expand the participation of those who do not participate at present. Questions of where it was offered, what was offered, why it was offered, what were the targets to be met and what penalties would be incurred if they were not met, would all take second place to the direct central question: Who are the missing participants which it is proposed to attract and how will they be attracted? Thus what is offered becomes less important than who is going to join in, and how it is offered becomes an open invitation to non-formal, informal learning to join whatever formal learning can offer and so become integral to lifelong learning.

Non-government organisations

It would then be open to voluntary bodies, trade unions and employers to seek public funding for schemes which sought to expand participation according to those criteria. LSCs and local education authorities between them could release local energy and initiative. House groups, housing estate groups, community groups, groups in the workplace could appoint development officers who worked on a high-risk basis in trying to shift the missing from absence to presence for participation. Voluntary organisations could deploy their long experience of doing just that until the combination of the vocational and transparency and accountability forced them into narrow lines of development. Always the condition for funding would be clear evidence that the scheme was designed to attract into lifelong learning some of the kinds of people who are non-participants and that there were reasonable grounds for expecting it to succeed in doing so.

If that style of flexible regime was established it is a reasonable assumption that as the word got around in voluntary organisations, some socially minded individuals who care about the condition of the country would seize the opportunity to put into practice some of the initiatives which have long been talked about and, in a modest way in some areas, have been acted upon. Voluntary bodies could create a ripple effect as one initiative led to another, where someone had sufficient energy and motivation. A neighbourhood group set up in a housing estate to work out how to improve security in the area – Making our Homes Safer – might result in one or two people thinking about following a formal course in the local FE college on home maintenance or personal budgeting or landscape gardening. The possibilities are endless if people who are capable of promoting lifelong learning and want to do so are enabled to put their sense of social responsibility to work without the need to play complicated bureaucratic games.

This line of thought is another way of saying that the combination of more supportive forms of reporting on the use of public funds would give more scope for charitable voluntary bodies to do what they do best: developing activities which formal state-funded institutions do not or cannot undertake, or operating independently of formal institutions.

The people who make up the personnel of voluntary bodies, both staff and members, constitute one of the most important groups of public servants the country has. Often they are not seen as such, but the public service they provide is of inestimable value. Releasing the potential energy which exists within those organisations is one of the more important ways of thinking about schemes for widening participation in lifelong learning.

Quite apart from anything else it could be a way of tapping one of the relatively untapped sources of support: the retired. It is often said that there is a teacher lurking in many people. The U3A is miles away from anything to do with recruiting the missing as participants in lifelong learning. However, just suppose that a flourishing U3A branch was contacted by a local development officer and asked if it had any members who would be willing to help promote a basic literacy and numeracy course as a neighbourhood activity in a poorer part of the town, all expenses paid, and fees and records to be looked after by the development officer. A free hand to see what could be done. If the approach was rejected, nothing would be lost; indeed, there might be gain, as some U3A members may be confronted with something they might not have come face to face with before. If it was accepted, lifelong learning would receive an additional boost for that area, and the U3A might become a developmental agency in its own right.

The same possibility exists in bodies such as the WEA. The underlying point is that the redesign of public accounting and accountability systems and an end to attempted control of the curriculum would act as a blood transfusion for voluntary bodies, urging them to move into a new phase of life. Government as enabler and not controller. Just as there was a social purpose in much of adult education between the two world wars and after offered by both voluntary and statutory bodies until the 1960s, so there would be a chance for voluntary organisations to reinforce that sense of social concern they have and capitalising on it as a main engine for their work. The government cannot do that. Rampant voluntary organisations might. Official bodies could then take up the baton when shown how to do it.

None of this is to suggest that there ought to be a free for all in spending public funds. Proposals for initiatives need the same degree of careful preparation as before. The difference is that allowances for a risk factor need to be incorporated in both approval procedures and financial regulations. The LSC has to follow all the procedures for financing the work of FE colleges, sixth-form colleges and voluntary bodies which it has inherited from Training and Enterprise Councils, the Further Education Funding Council and the DfES itself. The vital question is how far it can move towards the twin reforms referred to above. That will indicate how far trust is being reinstated.

Individuals

For individuals, the critical issue is for the government to reform, clarify and simplify the regulations for payment of fees and exemptions from them. Unless the present madness stops of urging people to join in and then throwing financial obstacles in their way to discourage if not prevent them from joining in, there is little hope of achieving the kinds of wider participation that are the key to success. Nor is it just a matter of fees. Childcare, transport and so on need to be made available for those in proven need of them. Doing so is a test of how deep or shallow is the public commitment to widening participation. However, unless the present plethora of entitlements is simplified those good intentions can never be realised. They put a premium on people having the motivation which is precisely what many have not got.

There is something else to say about those confusing rules concerning entitlements. The staff who have to deal with these issues in their day-to-day work in benefit offices also find them confusing. Under the stress of doing their best to cope with all the various issues which individuals present to them, it is inevitable that from time to time their patience snaps and anything which might be called good customer relations goes out through the window. This may deter those seeking their entitlements from going near the place again. It is bad enough for many to have to go there at all. To be treated brusquely adds to the resentment. And these are the very people who are among the missing and who need to be included if wider participation in LLL is to be achieved. So the confusion of regulations results in two intertwined deterrents.

The essential point about trust is ownership. It works at all levels. Members of a neighbourhood housing estate group are much more likely to be formed in the first place, let alone remain active, if they feel that they have chosen what they want to do. It belongs to them. It is not imposed on them. With luck they will become protective about it.

Similarly, public servants will be more enthusiastic about their work if they have some sense of being trusted to do it responsibly without heavy bureaucratic checks. They need to be trusted to take decisions. It is the same for voluntary bodies. About the worst way of getting the best service from them is to use procedures which seem to be based on the suspicion that somehow they might behave irresponsibly and misuse public funds. Autonomy needs to be restored to professionals, away from the pernicious over-emphasis on the line management philosophy of accountability. More trust, less pernickety oversight, more grown up. Being adult, no less.

What all this amounts to is a reminder that present arrangements for lifelong learning fail to recognise that all those concerned are adults and need to be treated in an adult way. As Mark Tennant and Philip Pogson put it in *Learning and Change in the Adult Years* (1995), 'adult education and adult development are inextricably bound up'. Whether as providers or participants, the reality of what it is to be adult needs to be the principle on which all schemes for lifelong learning are based. That means choice, responsibility and respect. The twin reforms referred to could offer a way of coming to terms with those requirements. For providers, and that includes government departments, it is no more than being a good employer.

The media

There is another area to be considered in the ways of actively encouraging widening participation in lifelong learning: the media.

One of the most extraordinary aspects of so many attempts by the government to get things done is the scant attention which is paid to the role of the media, particularly television. Getting things done in this context does not mean propaganda for particular political party policies, let alone the ghastly addiction to spin. How insulting that is in anything which tries to claim that it respects people living in an adult world. It is almost an invitation to ignore anything which is not outright entertainment.

To put the media in perspective there is the graphic phrase of Baroness

Greenfield, Director of the Royal Institution and Professor of Pharmacology in the University of Oxford. She talks about the people of the book and the people of the screen. This is not to imply that people of the book are unaffected by the screen. Of course they are. But when it comes to trying to recruit people for the public services, especially nursing and teaching, large numbers of the very people who are desperately needed to increase those numbers are now more likely to be people of the screen rather than people of the book. Thus serious recruitment initiatives ought to be working on the assumption that the television is the most effective way of trying to interest people in something which seems urgent to government, and the younger the generation the more likely this is to be the case. Yet whether it attempts to recruit nurses or teachers or to persuade people to take up vocational training, the government's TV adverts seem almost half-hearted with inadequate follow-up, as if it is an improper mode of addressing people; and some had limited success. Apart from the armed forces, which have no such qualms.

Applied to schemes for attracting the missing into lifelong learning, television and radio could be effective recruiters. The BBC is a public service broadcaster; its education service has a distinguished record. But now it ought to be a prime proponent of the practice, value and enjoyment of lifelong learning. Implicitly it is there in so many documentary and investigative programmes: time watch as an archaeological extravaganza; natural world programmes; historical series. But with some imagination someone could write a situation comedy about lifelong learning along the lines of *Educating Rita* but pitched at a different level. It could be a vehicle for all manner of information which would be of value to the missing. And if objections were based on fears of poor viewing rates as the price of mounting programmes with minority interests, if lifelong learning is as vital as the government says it is, then between them the Secretary of State and the BBC governors ought to find some way of exploiting the very systems which are available to them.

National Bureau for Current Affairs

Inspiration means some vision of better things, and better things means thinking about the well-being of society in general. Not that the government has ignored the ideas of the well-being of society in its efforts to promote further learning. Sometimes it has been explicit about just that. As mentioned above the drive for lifelong learning now has strands running through it which go beyond vocational and economic reasoning, and refer to additional learning in terms of the contribution it can make to the welfare of individuals, communities and the country at large.

When the current contributions of a whole range of public bodies are put together which could be exploited for the future, the list is impressive:

central and local government, universities and further education colleges, NIACE, open college networks, the WEA, National Trust, CAB, WI, U3A, not to mention professional bodies and especially trade unions. One way or another they are all engaged in some form of lifelong learning. The trouble is that it is all rather incoherent. Some connecting strand could make a world of difference.

During the later part of the Second World War there was an organisation called the Army Bureau of Current Affairs (ABCA). This was a government-funded education body intended to help armed service personnel – most of whom had only rudimentary schooling – to learn more about the society, country and the world in which they were going to live as civilians. Small twenty-page pamphlets were written by distinguished authorities on every aspect of what was then called current affairs. Economics and industry, politics, social issues and problems, foreign policy, every conceivable way of thinking about ways which could affect ordinary people's day-to-day lives were set down in straightforward plain English and made available widely through education officers. Sometimes there were compulsory classes, sometimes voluntary. Lifelong learning was not in the language then but retrospectively that is exactly what it was: liberal adult education. It was a deliberate attempt to equip returning ex-service personnel with some of the knowledge and skills they would need to re-enter a peacetime society which had changed beyond all recognition over those six years. ABCA was hugely successful. It was rather like the WEA writ large.

Returning soldiers, sailors and airmen were being helped deliberately to find their way into a new life in a new world. Now it is not so much society being faced with living in a new world, as living in an unending succession of baffling changes which characterise that world. The state of the country in the context of its highly technological nature, a growing international global economy, the declining influence which any government now has on the lives of its citizens, the widening gap between the relatively well-off and what are euphemistically called the poor, the fragmentation of society, and the decline of individual support systems whether through family, employment, church or community, all mean in effect that large numbers of people face a range of social problems which cause them great stress. And they are relatively new. Of course previous periods have seen the same sorts of tension arising because of changes in society. But now the tensions arising currently for so many people through almost every aspect of life, whether employment, travel, family and personal relations, home and personal security, pensions and ageing, bear down particularly hard on those who come within the missing bracket for lifelong learning. As a matter of social and ethical concern positive steps need to be taken to offer them constructive support.

Might there be an analogy between our own times and the immediate postwar period? Then the need was recovery. Now the need is regeneration. Perhaps now there should be an up-to-date version of ABCA to play a vital part in trying to promote lifelong learning as a means of understanding better the country and the world in which we live.

There is the European Union with far-reaching implications for individuals of either being in or out. Now terrorism has crept into international concerns in foreign policy along with overseas aid, crises of famine and wars in different parts of the world, and Northern Ireland has by no means settled into a stable peace. There are complicated issues of spare part surgery, of scientific research into possibilities of human cloning, of genetically modified foods. How to find somewhere to live for people in a first job has become a major issue. Uncertainties abound in the risk society. In all the present prosperity the promise of better things hangs invitingly, but for many it seems to slip away. For nearly fifty years social tensions were containable because the economic and social world was different. Now, with apparent political apathy, increasing extra-parliamentary participation, chronic housing problems, crime rates, all set in a rising tide of both general affluence and the growth of social inequality, there are open questions about the possibility of social unrest.

Perhaps there could be a National Bureau of Current Affairs. It could collect suitable materials from all manner of existing providers. The government itself, further and higher education would be a rich course, as would the WEA and other voluntary bodies. It could commission from the Institute of Public Policy Research, the Fabian Society, the Social Market Foundation, the Centre for Policy Studies, the Policy Studies Institute and others to produce new pamphlets written in plain English on special topics, chosen to explore some of the aspects of life which concerned people: safety and security; benefits, pension and ageing; health; family relationships; transport; international affairs; global corporations and so on. Each would be authoritative, unbiased and exploratory. Texts would be in print, on tape and on the Web. All would be available to any group or individual who wanted to use them whether formally or informally. Virtual reality classes could be held on TV and broadcast on radio. All formal education institutions and voluntary bodies and community groups, all local authorities, could make use of the materials as they chose. Libraries would have the pamphlets on their counters. The possibilities for engaging people as learners are almost limitless, provided that the topics were things which were either bothering them or of intrinsic interest to them. It could be a different way of promoting the development of citizenship education which is now part of the language in social concern.

Imagine a range of small publications with titles such as 'Why is public transport in such a mess?', 'Why is it so difficult for the NHS to meet public needs?', 'Why is teenage pregnancy so high?', 'What are the best ways for providing for old age?', 'What is the debate about genetically modified foods?', 'Where do cheap clothes come from?', 'What is serious about drug abuse?'

This could be a job for the LSC. Imagine it launching the whole series with a fanfare of publicity at a national meeting of all the key people including day-to-day practitioners, ensuring press and television coverage with an immediate set of TV programmes to show how the pamphlets were being used. As a National Bureau for Current Affairs the natural place to establish it would be NIACE. Imaginative leadership would give it a high profile. All access to and use of the materials would be free of charge. There would be no nonsense about a scheme which in x years was supposed to be self-supporting financially. Lifelong learning is too important for that. It needs to be seen in the same way as the NHS: a service too important to leave hanging in the breeze, a service which the government alone can provide.

What is more, the government should lead from the front for a change instead of playing staff officers in the rear. One of the most extraordinary aspects of the government's rhetoric about lifelong learning is that it does so little of it itself. There was once a wonderful incident in the MSC. A young civil servant, a high-flier who is now at the top of his tree, chaired a meeting for a project about WBL for employees. At the end of a discussion about finding employers who would join in the work, he observed that while the MSC talked a lot about employee training, it did nothing much about it. He announced that it, the MSC, would be one of the employers.

The government should heed that message. Of itself at present it does not do enough for the further learning of its own employees: it is high time that it did. The Cabinet Office could send out instructions to every department that in future it was to have an education officer who would make NBCA materials available and would be free to negotiate for office time to be devoted to appropriate topics for discussion.

If the government took the lead, it would be in a far stronger position when urging employers to be more active. It could be a way of tackling the pervasive culture among employers of non-participation in education and training. It could enable government to say look at what I do and not what I say. More important, osmosis could get to work. Imagine that if hundreds of pubic servants in central and local government were afforded the opportunity to consider some NBCA pamphlets in the employers' time, there would be an influence which would carry over into their day-to-day life. Most important, it would serve notice on the population that it was serious about lifelong learning. Leading by example it would encourage others to do likewise. Not least it would encourage workers in the field, seeking to engage the missing. It could give them a sense that they were part of a nationally recognised programme supported by government, something larger, rather than being left to work away somewhat isolated in their own little patch.

Objections to such a scheme would be legion, namely costs. But the costs of running such a national service would be marginal compared with many of the social costs which have to be met presently because of the predicament of many of the missing. The disappointing records of the Open Tech, the Open College and now the University of Industry will be quoted to say that similar attempts have been made already and that they have failed. Alternatively it will be said that much of it is done already through the University of Industry, individual colleges and universities, the WEA, the National Trust and the huge list of voluntary bodies who are active in this field, so why duplicate what is available already?

The point is that as a service it would not be duplication. As a national service available to everybody from trade unions to community and local groups, from large corporate employers to small businesses, public bodies such as local authorities, central government itself, the NHS, police and fire service as well as all kinds of formal providers, it could help create some global warming in the atmosphere for lifelong learning. It could even do something to help re-create some sense of cohesion by offering a small common denominator to further learning for all sorts and conditions of people. And all on a voluntary basis. And free.

Government learning representatives

The plea is for government to take a lead. It can so easily do so. It has already developed the means. All it has to do is to take as a model the union learning representative concept which it promoted itself and adapt it to providing a similar service to employees wherever they are. It could start by creating government learning representatives (GLRs) as front-line lifelong learning promoters, equipped with pamphlets produced under the auspices of the National Bureau of Current Affairs.

This would be an excellent model for promoting further learning in places of employment. It would be like lifelong learning on the hoof. Were the government to expand its ULR programme to cover other categories of employees it would be giving a lead in a way which no one else can. It would be rhetoric turned into positive encouragement and a significant move towards increasing the participation range in lifelong learning.

The government invented union learning representatives and can congratulate itself and the unions on making such a notable success of them. Now it can create its own government learning representatives. Suppose in every department and in each of its sections there was a Volunteer GLR. It is a fair guess that among civil servants and local government officers there would be a number of willing volunteers. And it is a fair guess that they would experience the same satisfaction from their role as do the

ULRs. Just a glance at the way the unions set out their stall for ULRs shows what a powerful influence GLRs could become.

An article in the TUC's publication *Learning with the Unions* lays out in diagram form how the role of a ULR has been conceived (Figure 7.1).

If the government put its weight behind such a development in the same way that unions grasped the possibility, there would be endless opportunities for promoting lifelong learning. Evidence from the ULRs makes clear that the volunteers gain great satisfaction from a sense of contributing to others. And if the union numbers mean what they seem to mean, then the volunteers are making a very good job of persuading their colleagues to take up some form of lifelong learning. If unions can do that why not government itself? If it did it would be a most convincing way of putting rhetoric into action. And promoting it could be another job for the Cabinet Office.

Figure 7.1

Source: By kind permission of the Trades Union Congress.

Student learning representatives/work-based learning for academic credit

Any Volunteers for the Good Society? is the title of a booklet published by the IPPR (Paxton and Nash 2002). It makes the case for offering students financial remissions of their fees in return for undertaking some volunteer work. This is something of a crib of the scheme which Bill Clinton introduced at the beginning of his presidency. In itself it is a good idea but it may be taken further in two directions, one of which would be of direct benefit to students and the other a contribution to the expansion of lifelong learning.

Work-based learning for academic credit is now a well-established element in higher education curricula and is becoming an increasing function of lifelong learning. The notion is that activities at work are not limited to those required by paid employment. Work as a place of learning can be in any practical activity through which it is possible to learn and not just putting in some time for work experience. Seen in those catholic terms there is an almost limitless range of possibilities for learning. Provided the 'work' activity is organised so as to enable a student to undertake a set of negotiated learning intentions which are acceptable in academic terms, then by using learning agreements students can gain academic credit through their work which is countable in a formal qualification. Hence it is possible to see student volunteering as earning both some remission of tuition fees and academic credit simultaneously.

This is one direction in which the IPPR's volunteering suggestions could be extended. The second is to connect volunteering with lifelong learning. Taking again the very successful way in which unions have exploited the possibilities offered by ULRs, with a little imagination a scheme could be developed whereby student volunteers who liked the idea could become student learning representatives (SLRs) assigned to a selected lifelong learning project. There are innumerable examples of the ways in which student unions in universities and colleges could undertake forms of community work. SLRs would add a strand to the structure of what they do already. Thus a student volunteer simultaneously could get remission from some fees, academic credit towards a university qualification and contribute to lifelong learning through engaging with approved programmes. It could also make a significant contribution to the overall notion of civic responsibility referred to earlier by Sir Harold Newby.

If further learning is as important as the government claims, not merely for economic reasons but for the well-being of society as a whole, and its importance is a prime theme of this book, then there have to be new ways of thinking to be deployed about the way adults learn and why they learn. Significant encouragement to achieve wider participation in lifelong learning has to begin with the government acting so as to release initiative and imagination by loosening its grip at the centre.

It would be interesting to know if those who thought up the scheme for union learning representatives had any vision about their potential as an engine for the general expansion of learning. As it is, the government has such an engine waiting for development. It could be a way of mobilising lifelong learning in a way which was open to no other initiative. It could even be a move towards that much talked-of and rather nebulous concept: a learning society.

So if the doing it is to get anywhere near the widening participation which everyone agrees is desirable, there need to be new approaches from the government down. The government has to decrease micro-management to release initiatives. It needs to facilitate flexible terms of employment. At the same time it needs to lead from the front by putting weight behind its contributions to the lifelong learning of its own employees. Union learning representatives show what a new approach can produce. Perhaps student learning volunteers and adult learning volunteers could find a place in those initiatives. The balance in lifelong learning needs to be tilted from economic concerns to wider issues of social well-being. Trying to do so will be inevitably uncomfortable for some people, contentious even and resisted. That will be the price of having lifelong learning which will fit the twenty-first century.

Chapter 8

Postscript

Making sense of lifelong learning

Lifelong learning needs to be seen as a vital part of attempts at the regeneration of British society. After fifteen years of malign neglect came five years of rather timid government. That timidity is not surprising. An inexperienced collection of ministers were full of good intentions about repairing the damage visited on the country by the Tories as they underfunded public services or privatised where they could. Only later were those good intentions matched with a full realisation of the extent to which that underfunding had affected the very fabric of society. After its many efforts between 1997 and 2002 New Labour then braced itself to be more energetic in its efforts to revitalise the public services.

Simultaneously with that underfunding went a steady widening of the gap between the growing numbers of people who are relatively, if not well-off, and the alarming numbers who are on the poverty line if not below it. Columnists claim that whereas in 1979 when the Thatcher government took office, 9 per cent lived below the poverty line in 2000, three years into the first Labour government the figure had risen to 25 per cent. Likewise, while the current rate for unemployment is £53.05 a week, if it had kept pace with the 1979 figure the figure would be £87, and pensions would be £107.04 as equivalent to the 1979 figure. It is £98. 'This is only one sign of how hard Labour has had to run just to catch up with 25 year ago' (Polly Toynbee, *Guardian*, 5 June 2002). Catch-up again. If these figures convince people of nothing else, they show how strong is the need for lifelong learning to relate to social inclusion and citizenship.

This is the context for lifelong learning. Never mind the importance of having sufficient skilled IT and production staff; here are social issues of deeply worrying dimensions. Somehow lifelong learning needs to address both, and that means outreach programmes in a diversity of ways which have not been seen and can only be guessed at. Enterprise through entrepreneurs needs to create adult versions of lifelong learning provision. That can only be done by altering the balance between top-down and bottom-up activities. Top-down has to stop its domination. Bottom-up has to be given the freedom to use its imagination. Professionals and their expertise have to be brought back into the front line of activities. As long as top-down is characterised by funding according to predetermined numbers of qualifications there is little space for imagination. The government has to learn to get out of the way.

In our very complex, shifting society one of the main difficulties is, as Ken Brown puts it: 'education takes place in an atmosphere of inevitable uncertainty about ends and means. But this very lack of certainty has implications for the ways in which a society views learning and organises teaching' (Brown 2002).

Just as the government needs to listen carefully to professionals so it needs to listen to the voluntaries. Successful though such organisations are in attracting all manner of adult learners, they would go out of business if they tried a heavy-handed top-down approach. They thrive because they work with their potential students or volunteers to decide what it is that people would like to learn more about. It is the WEA members who decide what courses or opportunities they want to learn. That bottom-up style combines with tutors' advice as top-down provision, but it is advice, not prescription.

Ford's EDAP committees were successful in increasing significantly the number of employees who joined the rank of the learners, because they responded to requests from their colleagues. There was no attempt to tell people what they ought to learn. Union learning representatives are another success story. Volunteers talk with fellow members to encourage participation in lifelong learning, offer advice as to how to find the best way of doing so and support individuals in making those efforts. No one tells anyone what to do. They do it and get on with it. Bottom-up.

There was no need to talk about commitment to learning, or attitudes to learning, the true purpose of learning or motivation for learning, or any other of these pious mouthings, because at a personal level choice meant that all or some of those motivations came into play for each individual. And for each individual the combination would be unique. The ages and stages of adulthood were implicitly being taken into full account.

For no other group is that more important than for young people. All the pressures from the marketing and consumer world beam out the notion of choice, and on the basis of that presumed choice in one way or another they are being encouraged to develop what they feel to be their own individuality, leaving them to do the best they can to make sense of the world as they see it. But their motivation for learning or lack of it resides in choice, and to provide them with a choice of learning which feels real to them means finding out what they would like to know more about and then finding ways of responding positively. They will choose to learn or not to learn at different stages of their lives as mundane matters of domesticity, security and continuity take over from worries about self-esteem which ran through peer group experience. But whatever the timing they will only choose to learn for one of two reasons: if, from school, parents, relatives and friends, they have the idea that learning need not necessarily be boring but there is some point to it, or because some unavoidable need to learn confronts them. If neither applies then they become part of the drifting missings. That throws down the challenge to schools and colleges.

Here enticing them to choose is the key. It is a form of student-generated curriculum. Not some pre-ordained syllabus but taking their choice seriously of what they would like to learn. This can be the first step to convincing them that they are not the poor learners which, alas, is what so many end up thinking of themselves as a result of their school experience. Learning something which they want to know about can change attitudes to learning. They need the opportunity to do so. This is no more than the best approaches to the older adults among the cohorts of the missing. But for the young it is hard to see what might work more effectively.

One of the most important aspects of those forms of working such as the voluntaries or EDAP is that essentially they are democratic. Since one of the most worrying aspects of the missing from lifelong learning is that so many are actually socially excluded or feel themselves to be excluded, any activity which encourages them to join in some activity which might make them feel included is vital in its own right. Whether any such activity leads to learning which has an economic justification is almost beside the point. Learning to join in an enterprise with others and to take some responsibility for it is a form of social learning which is far more important for the missing than NVQs in anything. They may follow, but they should not come first unless that is what people actually want. The structure of lifelong learning needs to take account of that.

This is where Hoggart's plea for what he calls critical literacy comes in. People can be technically literate in reading, writing and number or basic skills as they have been labelled without being functionally literate as whole persons. No further bits of initiative-itis will do anything to correct that balance. Engagement in some bottom-up activity would help to correct that balance. Moreover, because one of the best ways of encouraging people to improve their basic skills is when they realise that they need them in order to do something that they want to do, bottom-up experience can become a route to getting a better grip on the basics without setting out explicitly to do so.

So the country needs devolution with executive power given to institutions to develop how they decide to set about the task, within agreed block allocation budgets and without ring-fenced funds. There needs to be some alteration to the contractual terms for people working in this field. There needs to be an intelligent public accounting system designed to support and facilitate local initiative rather than obstructing it. The benefits system has to be simplified again in ways which support and encourage individuals rather than deter them. Above all it needs a different set of attitudes about institutions and within them to re-tune them so that their public service role takes full account of the society they are there to serve, especially adults. They need to be adult for adults living in an adult world, and all that applies to a far wider range of activity than lifelong learning. It points to the need for a joined-up government which works. Many of the issues surrounding lifelong learning are those which touch other social policies and initiatives.

However, it is important to hold tight to the proposition that lifelong learning is an aspiration and not a policy. That does not make it any less important that it should be prominent as a reference point for what needs to be done about increasing the numbers of people who are active learners. In his book *Lifelong Learning and the New Educational World* (2000) John Field makes three comments on this. He says that it indicates an aspiration for the capacity to cope with change and choice as well as the need for additional skills as tools to do so. He claims that lifelong learning as a concept relates to changes in the patterns of individual behaviour. And then there is a warning. For lifelong learning can become a mechanism for exclusion and control. Things are fine for those who are within its parameters but those who are outside the lifelong learning network now run risks of losing support from the state as the government makes pronouncements about extending the loss of benefits for twenty-six weeks for those who refuse either employment or training.

But if it not a policy, lifelong learning may be seen as a tool for tackling all sorts of social and economic problems. Through imaginative schemes it can be a vehicle for carrying a better understanding of benefit systems, housing, drug abuse, crime, if, that is, some of the missing can be enticed to become participants. For some of the missing it could become lifelong learning for lifelong living.

Exploring some of the issues to be dealt with in achieving wider participation exposes many of the problems running right through society. And while there may be an argument which says that despite its good intentions the government has helped create some of those problems, there is no doubt that reversing its centralising tendency, which is one of the strong themes running through this book, is needed across wide tracks of public life. As has been said, the problem is to steer a complex society without suffocating it. It turns out therefore that making sense of lifelong learning is part of making better sense of the society we live in. There was a time when that was what lifelong learning was for. Perhaps it is just returning to its origins.

References

ACACE (1982) *Continuing Education from Policies to Practice*, Advisory Council for Adult and Continuing Education, Leicester.

Ball, Sir Christopher and Coffield, F. (1999) 'Our learning society', debate, *RSA Journal*, December.

Beinart, S. and Smith, P. (1997) *National Adult Learning Survey*, Research Report No. 49, London: HMSO.

Brighouse, T. (2002) 'How many are to be successful?', in *Education: Putting It Right*, October, www.RSA.org/Read.

Brown, K. (2002) *The Right to Learn: Alternatives for a Learning Society*, London: RoutledgeFalmer.

Carter, Sir Charles (1996) 'Recognising the value of informal learning', lecture to the Learning from Experience Trust.

Chickering, A.W. and Havighurst, R.J. (1981) *Responding to the New Realities of Diverse Students and a Changing Society*, London: Jossey Bass.

Delors, J. (1997) Preface, in R. Fryer, *Learning – The Treasure Within*, London: HMSO.

Demos (2002) Wilkinson, A. and Mygian, R.

DES (1963) *Half our Future* (Newsom Report), London: HMSO.

—— (1973) *Adult Education: A Plan for Development* (Russell Report), London: HMSO.

DfEE (1996) *Learning to Compete: Education and Training for 14 to 19*, Green Paper CMD 3486, London: HMSO.

—— (1997a) *Report of the National Committee of Enquiry into Higher Education: Higher Education in the Learning Society*, London: HMSO.

—— (1997b) *Learning Works: Widening Participation in Further Education* (Kennedy Report), London: HMSO.

—— (1997c) *Learning and Working Together for the Future*, London: HMSO.

—— (1998a) *The Learning Age: A New Renaissance for a New Britain*, Green Paper CMD 3790, London: HMSO.

—— (1998b) *Learning and Working Together for the Future: A Strategic Framework for 2002*, London: HMSO.

—— (1998c) *Individual Learning Accounts*, London: HMSO.

—— (1998d) *Union Learning Fund: A Partnership in Lifelong Learning*, London: HMSO.

—— (1999) *Learning to Succeed – A New Framework for Post-16+ Learning*, White Paper CMD 4392, London: HMSO.

Erikson, E. (1950) *Childhood and Society*, New York: W.W. Norton.

Field, J. (2000) *Lifelong Learning and the New Educational World*, Stoke-on-Trent: Trentham Books.

Hargreaves, D (1997) 'Guru predicts classroom exodus', *Times Educational Supplement*, 30 May.

Havighurst, R.J. (1972) *Developmental Tasks and Education*, New York: McKay.

Henry, P. and Mumford, A. (1992) *Manual of Learning Styles*, Maidenhead: P. Henry

Hillage, J., Uden, T., Aldridge, F. and Eccles, J. (2000) *Adult Learning in England: A Review*, London: Institute for Employment Studies and the National Institute for Adult Continuing Education.

Hoggart, R. (1992) *An Imagined Life*, Oxford: Oxford University Press.

—— (1995) *The Way We Live Now*, London: Chatto & Windus.

Holford, J. (1994) *Union Education in Britain: A TUC Activity*, University of Nottingham: Department of Adult Education.

Jessup, F.W. (1969) *Lifelong Learning: A Symposium of Continuing Education*, London: Pergamon Press.

Kolb, D. (1976) *Learning Styles Inventory*, Boston, MA: McBer and Co.

LET (2000) *Mapping APEL: Accreditation of Prior Experiential Learning in English Higher Education*, Learning from Experience Trust.

—— (2002) *Action Learning in the Community*, Learning from Experience Trust.

McGivney, V. (1990) *Working with Excluded Groups*, London: National Institute for Adult Continuing Education.

—— (1999) *Informal Learning in the Community*, London: National Institute for Adult Continuing Education.

Marshall, T.H. (1991) *Citizenship and Social Class*, London: Pluto Press. First published 1950.

Miller, A. (1969) 'First Things First', in F.W. Jessup (ed.) *Lifelong Learning: A Symposium of Continuing Education*, London: Pergamon Press.

Myers, B. (2001) 'Which America will we be now?, *The Nation*, November.

NAGCELL (1927) *Learning for the Twenty-first Century*, First report of the National Advisory Group for Continuing Education and Lifelong Learning.

—— (1999) *Creating Learning Cultures: Next Steps in Achieving the Learning Age*, Second report of the National Advisory Group for Continuing Education and Lifelong Learning.

Newby, Sir Howard (2002) Statement at the conference, 'The future of higher education – help us share it', April.

NIACE (2002) *Survey of Participation*, London: NIACE.

OECD (1995) *Making Lifelong Learning a Reality for All*, Paris: OECD.

O'Neill, O. (2002) 'A question of trust', Reith Lectures, London: BBC.

Paxton, W. and Nash, V. (2002) *Any Volunteers for the Good Society?*, IPPR.

PCS (2002) 'Our time', *PCS Journal*, 15 (6), pp. 42–4.

Rogers, J. (2001) *Adult Learning* (4th edn), Buckingham: Open University Press.

Ryan, A. (1999) *Liberal Anxieties and Liberal Education: What is Education Really For and Why it Matters*, London: Prospect Books.

Sanderson, B. (2002) 'Unleashing the tiger: will education and training transform the UK?', *RSA Journal*, 3 June, pp. 48–53

Sheehy, G. (1996) *New Passages*. London: HarperCollins.

Smethurst, R. (1995) 'Education: a public or private good', *RSA Journal*, December.

Tennant, M. and Pogson, P. (1995) *Learning and Change in the Adult Years*, London: Jossey Bass.

Thomas, R. Murray (1972) *Human Development Theories*, Thousand Oaks, Calif.: Sage Publications.

Tomlinson, S. (2001) *Education in a Post Welfare Society*, Oxford: Oxford University Press.

TUC (2002a) *The Quiet Revolution: The Rise of the Union Representatives*, London: Trades Union Congress.

—— (2002b) *The Learning Gap*, London: Trades Union Congress.

Index

A and AS levels 137
Action Learning in the Community 110
Advisory Committee on Adult and
    Continuing Education 23–4
Army Bureau of Current Affairs 20, 149
assessment of prior experiential
    learning (APEL) 16, 18, 39, 41, 54,
    64
Association of Teachers in Colleges and
    Departments of Education 116
Association of Technical training
    Institutions 116
Association of University Teachers 117
Association of Women and Male
    Teachers 117

Baker, Kenneth 72
Ball, Sir Christopher 28, 29
Basic Skills Agency 53
Beacon Schools 10
Blunkett, David 31, 93
BBC Good Food Magazine 14
Brighouse, Tim 131, 133–4
British Medical Association 104
Brown, Ken 157
Browning, David 41

Cabinet Office 128, 151, 153
Callaghan, Jim 72
Cambridgeshire Village Colleges 21
Careers Service 49
Carter, Sir Charles 5, 15
Chickering, A. 85
Churchill, Sir Winston 19, 26
Citizens Advice Bureau 43–4, 79
Citizen's Charter 59
Clarke, Kenneth 72
Coffield, Frank 29, 95

Council for National Academic Awards
    16

Dearing Report 30, 93
Delors, Jacques 31
Department for Education and
    Employment 28, 31–4
Department for Education and Skills
    37, 100, 118, 128
Department of Employment 16
Department of Transport 97
Department for Work and Pensions 128

Eccles, David 72
EdExcel 41, 56
Education Permanente 22–3
Elliott, John 11
Employee Development and Assistance
    Programme 123–4, 125–6, 157–8
Erikson, E.H. 83
European Commission 141
European Year of Lifelong Learning 5
Excellence in Cities 10

Field, John 91, 120, 131–2, 134, 143, 159
Ford, UK 123
Fryer, Bob 31, 53
Foundation Degree 9, 35, 132
Further Education Colleges 9, 24, 57,
    139
Further Education Development
    Agency 25
Further Education Funding Council 37

General Certificate of Secondary
    Education 137–8
General National Vocational
    Qualifications 72

Goldsmiths College 5, 24, 110, 141
Government Learning Representatives
    152
Greenfield, Baroness Susan 148

Hampden Jackson, John 21
Hargreaves, David 95–6
Havighurst, R.J. 84,
Henry and Mumford 89
Higher Education Funding Council
    100, 141
Higher and Further Education Act
    1992 26
Higher National Diploma 141
Hodge, Margaret 108
Hoggart, Richard 19, 21, 24, 25, 26, 51,
    158
Horsburgh, Florence 19
Humanities Curriculum Project 11,
    138

Individual Learning Accounts 38
Institute of Employment Studies 64
Institute of Personnel Development 49

Jacques, Frank 21
James, Lord of Rusholme 116
Joseph, Sir Keith 24, 25

Kennedy Report 30, 92
Kent Training and Enterprise Council
    126
Kolb, David 89

Learning and Skills Council 9, 16, 36,
    50–1, 65, 67, 93–4, 97, 100, 141, 143–4
Learning from Experience Trust 16,
    110
Local Education Authorities 21, 26,
    48–9, 143
Loevinger, J. 87
London Metropolitan University 141

Macdonald, Barry 11
McGivney, Veronica 64, 65, 114–15
MacMaster University 65, 66, 91
Manpower Services Commission 102,
    143
Mansbridge, Alfred 20, 31
Marshall, T.H. 138–9
Morris, Henry 21
Myers, Bill 112

National Adult Learning Survey 64–5
National Advisory group for
    Continuing and Lifelong Learning
    31, 69–70, 74–5, 106
National Association of Teachers in
    Further and Higher Education 116,
    117
National Bureau for Current Affairs
    150–1
National Council for Vocational
    Qualifications 9, 26, 27–8, 36, 56, 107
National Curriculum 10, 72, 77, 138
National Extension College 49
National Institute for Adult and
    Continuing Education 25, 41, 49, 91,
    120, 151
National Open College Network 41
National Training Organisation for
    Arts Entertainment and Cultural
    Heritage 35
National Trust 44–5, 79
National Union of Teachers 117
Neighbourhood Watch 79
Newby, Sir Howard 109, 111, 154
Newsom Report, *Half our Future* 11

Ofsted 10
O'Neill, Onora 103–4
Open College 9, 25, 36, 40, 41
Open Tech 9, 36
Open University 49, 56, 60
Organisation for Economic
    Cooperation and Development 30,
    53, 54, 81

Pogson, Philip 147
Prince's Trust 11
Professional, industrial and commercial
    updating 25

Regional Skills Councils 9
Reith Lectures 103–4
Return to Employment Plan 26
Robertson, David 132
Rogers, Carl 90
Royal Society of Arts 28, 41
Ruddock, Jean 11
Ruskin College 72
Russell Report 23–4, 31
Ryan, Alan 101

Sanderson, Bryan 50, 67

Schools Council 137
Sheehy, Gail 86–7, 94
Smethurst, Richard 28
Smithers, Alan 131, 134–5
Social Exclusion 42
Speaker's Commission on Citizenship 138
Stenhouse, Lawrence 11, 138
Student Learning Representatives 154

Tawney, R.H. 16, 20, 31
Tennant, Mark 147
Thatcher, Margaret 23, 24, 116
Tomlinson, Sally 14
Toynbee, Polly 156
Trade Unions 39–40, 58
Training and Enterprise Councils 9, 36, 80, 97
Treasury 128, 142–3

Union Learning Fund 39
Union Learning Representatives 40, 58, 124, 125, 153

Unit for the Development of Adult and Continuing Education 25
Universities 50–1
University Extension Movement 20
University of Industry 9
University of the Third Age 46–7, 57, 97, 145
Universities Vocational Award Council 56, 80

Vocational Qualifications Awards Service 56
Voluntary Sector National Training Organisation 35

Wagner, Leslie 80
Weldon, Fay 139
Williams, Raymond 21
Williams, Shirley 23, 102
Women's Institute 45–6, 79
Work-based Learning 16
Workers Education Association (WEA) 19, 42–3, 97, 110, 129, 146